Essays on Mammals of Białowieża Forest

Essays on Mammals of Białowieża Forest

Edited by

Bogumiła JĘDRZEJEWSKA and Jan Marek WÓJCIK

MAMMAL RESEARCH INSTITUTE
POLISH ACADEMY OF SCIENCES
Białowieża

2004

Copyright @ 2004
by Mammal Research Institute, Polish Academy of Sciences

Published by Mammal Research Institute
Polish Academy of Sciences
17-230 Białowieża, Poland

All rights reserved. No part of this publication may be reproduced, stored in a retrieval system, or transmitted, in any form or by any means, electronic, mechanical, photocopying, recording, or otherwise, without the prior permission of the copyright owner.

ISBN 83-907521-1-5

Cover photo by Jan Walencik.

Published by Mammal Research Institute, Polish Academy of Sciences in the frames of project BIOTER – Centre of Excellence in Biodiversity Conservation and Mammal Research, financed by the European Commission under the Fifth Framework Programme (contract EVK2-CT-2002-80011), Key Action "Global Change, Climate and Biodiversity" within the Energy, Environment and Sustainable Development Programme.
Project co-ordinator at EC's DGResearch: dr Martin Sharman
Project co-ordinator at MRI PAS: prof. dr Włodzimierz Jędrzejewski

Typeset by Mammal Research Institute,
Polish Academy of Sciences, 17-230 Białowieża, Poland

Printed and bound in Poland
INTROPACK Jerzy Iwaniuk

Contents

1. Introduction
   B. Jędrzejewska and J. M. Wójcik ... 1
2. Białowieża Primeval Forest – a treasure and a challenge
   B. Jaroszewicz ... 3
3. Biodiversity of forest mammals
   K. Stachura, M. Niedziałkowska and K. Bartoń ... 13
4. European bison – history of a flagship species
   Z. Pucek ... 25
5. Life of the European bison
   M. Krasińska and Z. A. Krasiński ... 35
6. Mating systems of ungulates
   K. Daleszczyk ... 43
7. Red deer – a tale of two deer
   J. F. Kamler, B. Jędrzejewska and S. Miścicki ... 51
8. Life after death – scavenging on ungulate carcasses
   N. Selva ... 59
9. The brown bear – a story without a happy ending
   T. Samojlik ... 69
10. Wolves' predation on deer
    W. Jędrzejewski and B. Jędrzejewska ... 77
11. The large cat in Europe
    K. Schmidt ... 85
12. Badgers – digging after earthworms
    R. Kowalczyk ... 93
13. The versatile pine martens
    A. Zalewski ... 103

14. Weasel – hard life of a small predator
    K. Zub — 111

15. Bats in trees
    I. Ruczyński — 121

16. Seed crops and forest rodents
    B. Jędrzejewska, Z. Pucek and W. Jędrzejewski — 129

17. Voles in river valleys
    J. Gliwicz and E. Jancewicz — 139

18. Natural economy of mammalian energy budgets
    M. Konarzewski — 149

19. Competition and coexistence of shrews
    L. Rychlik — 161

20. Common shrews – chromosome races and evolution
    J. M. Wójcik — 171

21. Genetic diversity of mammals
    M. Tokarska, A. M. Wójcik and J. M. Wójcik — 181

22. Morphometrics of mammals – the scientific success of teeth
    E. Szuma — 191

23. Mammal Research Institute in Białowieża
    K. Niedziałkowski — 197

Appendix — 203

Authors' profiles and addresses — 209

1

Introduction

With about 4,260 extant species, mammals are not the most diverse animals on the planet. They are outnumbered not only by an unchallenged variety of invertebrates (for instance, 1 million species of insects and 80 thousand species of molluscs), but by other groups of vertebrates as well (9,700 species of birds and about 25,000 species of fishes). Yet mammals are the animals with which humans have had the most profound, affectionate association.

In this book, in over 20 essays, a group of scientists share their fascination with and knowledge of wild mammals. The authors are scientists from the Mammal Research Institute of the Polish Academy of Sciences in Białowieża, which celebrated the 50th anniversary of its foundation in 2002, as well as scientists from other institutes or universities, who cooperate with MRI staff in joint projects. The personal touch, added to the objective scientific information presented in this book, stems from the fact that each author has written on her or his favourite species or biological problem, to which they have devoted years of hard work.

Many of the studies featured were conducted in the Białowieża Primeval Forest that has long held the title of the best preserved temperate forest in the European lowlands. The woodlands of Białowieża harbour a great diversity of mammals, from rare forest bats, shrews and small rodents, to a beast of ancient times – the European bison. Breath-takingly beautiful in itself, the primeval forest of Białowieża is also an important reference point for studies done in other ecosystems on our continent altered by human activity.

Essays on Mammals of Białowieża Forest are primarily intended as an educational resource for Polish and foreign students, who come to the Mammal Research Institute to learn about ecology, biodiversity, genetics, evolution, and conservation biology of mammals. But, we hope that other readers – professional biologists, conservationists, naturalists, and outdoorsmen – will also enjoy discovering the new information on common and rare species.

By writing about mammals in their natural environment, we not only aim to raise the reader's appreciation for the beauty and diversity of life, but also his or her concern about species in danger of disappearing forever. Since records of animal species have been kept, nearly 90 species of mammals have already become extinct globally, and about 240 are critically endangered. Scientists are not usually in a position of power to halt the destruction of biodiversity, yet – as exemplified by the case of the European bison – clear knowledge on the vanishing species and their habitats is a prerequisite for successful conservation.

This book was prepared as part of the activities of the Centre of Excellence in Biodiversity Conservation and Mammal Research in European Terrestrial Ecosystems – BIOTER established at the Mammal Research Institute. The project (contract no: EVK2-CT-2002-80011 for years 2002–2005) is supported by the European Commission under the Fifth Framework Programme and contributing to the implementation of the Key Action "Global Change, Climate and Biodiversity" within the Energy, Environment and Sustainable Development Programme. The book forms a deliverable 1.5 of the Work Package 1.

Many of the research projects described were supported by grants from the budget of the Mammal Research Institute of the Polish Academy of Sciences, the Polish Committee of Scientific Research (PCSR) and other national and foreign foundations in 1991–2003. The most recent grants from the PCSR are acknowledged by Katarzyna Daleszczyk (grant no. 6 P04G 057 21), Joanna Gliwicz (6 P04F 036 15 and 3 P04F 043 22), Bogumiła Jędrzejewska and Stanisław Miścicki (5 P06H 034 18), Ireneusz Ruczyński (3 P04F 008 22), Leszek Rychlik (6 P04F 036 21), and Karol Zub (3 P04F 051 25). The work on a chapter by Włodzimierz Jędrzejewski was supported by Euronatur (Germany), Jan F. Kamler by the Polish-U.S. Fulbright Commission, Magdalena Niedziałkowska by the 5. FP's project BioPlatform (contract no. EVK2-CT-2001-20009), and Krzysztof Schmidt by the Directorate General of the State Forests. The chapter by Jan M. Wójcik is based on long-term collaboration with Jeremy B. Searle (University of York, Great Britain). The Directors of the Białowieża National Park, as well as the Białowieża, Browsk and Hajnówka Forestry Districts kindly granted us the permission to conduct field studies in Białowieża Primeval Forest.

We express our sincere gratitude to students and volunteers at the MRI, Celine Perchellet (University of Kansas, U.S.A.), Leila Brook (University of Melbourne, Australia), and Stephanie Prior-Tischbier (University of Strathclyde, Great Britain), who did a great job of polishing the English language in the text. We sincerely thank the photographers, whose pictures enliven this book. Karol Zub prepared most of the figures in the CorelDraw programme, Tomasz Kamiński and Tomasz Samojlik edited the electronic versions of the photos, and dr Piotr Daszkiewicz translated the historical sources to Chapter 9 from French. Antonina Świerszcz performed the computer type-setting of the book. The final product owes much to her skills and creative attitude. Finally, we thank all the authors for their efforts and willingness to complete the task in a short time. It has been a great pleasure to work in such a competent team.

Bogumiła Jędrzejewska
Jan M. Wójcik

Białowieża, April 2004

2

Białowieża Primeval Forest
– a treasure and a challenge

Bogdan Jaroszewicz

In the lowlands of the European temperate zone, only a few patches of old-growth woodlands survive close to a natural state. One of these remnants is Białowieża Primeval Forest, the heritage of past generations. Will we succeed in preserving it for our descendants?

Ancient forest

The Białowieża Primeval Forest, a temperate woodland of 1500 square kilometers, is located on vast, East-European plains, near the watershed of the Black and the Baltic Seas. The history and development of plant cover in the Forest dates back to the retreat of the Baltic Glaciation, 10–12 thousand years ago. Although the glacier had not covered the area of the contemporary forest, its influence on the climate was strong enough to create cold steppes with their characteristic megafauna, the mammoths, giant deer, woolly rhinoceros, steppe bison, and cave lions.

With the recession of the Glacial period, the land became covered with pioneering trees such as pine and birch, and the large mammals disappeared. During the following millenia the climate warmed up to reach the optimum in the Atlantic period (5,500–2,500 BC). This time was marked by the formation of rich, deciduous forests containing oak, hornbeam, lime, elm, ash, and maple. Later the climate became cooler, allowing spruce to invade the forests. By about 2,000 BC, the treestands of Białowieża were already similar to what we see nowadays in the natural, old-growth forests of the Białowieża National Park (Photo 2.1).

The first traces of human presence date back to Neolithic times. Between 100–300 AD, the region of Białowieża Forest was sparsely populated by the Goths, on their migration from the Baltic to the Black Sea. Slavic tribes left archaeologically perceptible signs since 600 AD, but within the contemporary range of Białowieża Forest, their inhabitation has been proven from the 11th century. Since then, the Białowieża Forest region has been the place where the Eastern and Western Slavic influences meet and coexist.

In medieval times, the region of Białowieża Forest was located on the borderland of the Kievan Rus and the Piast Poland. It has long suffered frequent periods of unrest, and raids by these two neighbours, as well as by the Balts from Jatwiez and Lithuania. Finally, in the 14th century the region was incorporated into the Grand Duchy of Lithuania, and the Forest itself became a private land, inherited by the Lithuanian rulers. With the formation of the Polish-Lithuanian

Photo 2.1. Most common forest associations of Białowieża Forest: oak-lime hornbeam stands (upper left), wet alder-ash forest (right), and pine-spruce forest (lower left). Photos by Paweł Fabijański.

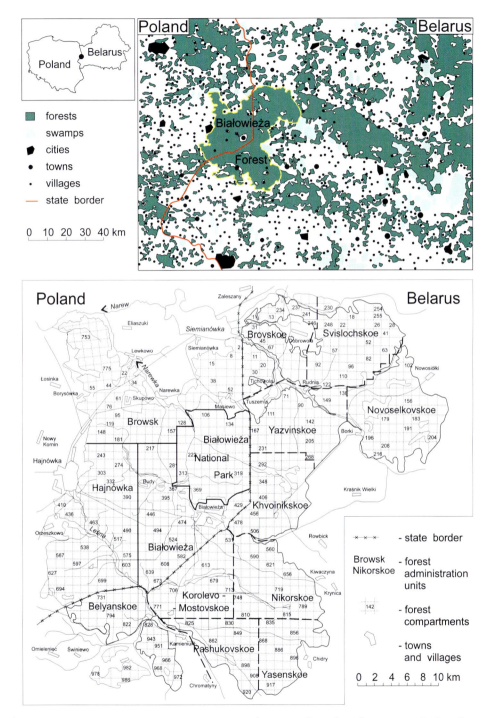

Figure 2.1. Białowieża Forest among the woodlands of eastern Poland and western Belarus Republic (upper graph), and a schematic map of Białowieża Forest with division into forest administration units (lower graph). (Reprinted from: *Predation in vertebrate communities*. Springer Verlag, Berlin, 1998; modified.)

Commonwealth, in the late 14th century, the Forest gained the title of royal woodland, protected against uncontrolled settlement and exploitation, and used mainly for monarchial hunts (see Chapters 4 and 9).

Already in the 16th century, forest services were established. They included the stationing of over 100 guards settled in small villages around the Forest. These professional forest and game wardens enjoyed hereditary posts, had higher social ranking than villeins, and were provided with land and privileges. Their main duties were to watch for European bison and other large game, organise the monarchial hunts, and strictly control the exploitation of forest resources. This system of protection grew to include nearly 300 people, and until the end of the 18th century, it was an efficient barrier against colonisation and overexploitation of the Forest.

In 1795, Poland lost its independence, and the region of Białowieża Forest fell under Russian rule. The former system of protection gradually declined, but nonetheless Białowieża Forest retained the status of state woodland, and European bison continued to be protected. In the late 19th century, the Russian czars became interested in hunting in the Forest, and as such Białowieża Forest became the czars' property and hunting ground from 1888. The 'modern' rules of protection included the control of large predators (see Chapters 9 and 10), and promotion of ungulates, especially by ample winter feeding. Despite protection, human pressure on the Forest increased, with large-scale pasturing of cattle in the woods, modest exploitation of timber, a denser network of settlements, and the czar's monumental hunting palace being built in Białowieża village, in place of the former wooden mansion of Polish kings before 1795.

Today's forest

The current status and system of management of Białowieża Forest is rooted in the political events of the early 20th century. The First World War ended the 120-year long Russian rule over Białowieża Forest. The few years of German occupation brought disastrous exploitation of timber and decimation of all game species, including the European bison (see Chapter 4). After World War I, when the Republic of Poland regained independence, the woodlands of Białowieża became commercial, state forests. Only a small area was protected in 1921 as the Forest District Reserve, and later it developed into Białowieża National Park (47 km^2). The remaining woodlands were undergoing timber exploitation by the Polish State Forestry, and also temporarily, between 1924–1929, by the English company "Century European Timber Corporation".

Despite its rather small size, from the very beginning Białowieża National Park has had a strong, positive influence on development in the region. Based on the national park's infrastructure, its first directors Prof. Józef Paczoski and Prof. Jan J. Karpiński initiated and developed environmental education programmes and scientific research, and created the natural history museum and show reserve of the recently recovered European bison. The number of tourists visiting the Park increased from 2,000 in 1925, to over 47,000 in January–August 1939.

During the Second World War, Białowieża Forest was initially under Soviet occupation (1939–1941). The Soviet rulers continued and indeed, intensified the exploitation of timber. With the Nazis invading Białowieża in 1941, the Forest became the Hunting Ground of the Third Reich (Reichjagdgebiet), and exploitation ceased. In 1945, the new state border between Poland and the Soviet Union, specifically the Belarussian Soviet Socialist Republic, divided the Białowieża Forest into two parts (Figure 2.1).

The Polish section of the Forest, in total about 600 km^2 or 40% of the Forest's area, had conserved the pre-war scenario, with the small, protected Białowieża National Park, surrounded by stands that were commercially exploited and replanted. The Park continued to attract visitors and scientists. From the 1930's to 1952, three scientific institutions were established in the village: the Natural Forests Department of the Forestry Research Institute, the Geobotanical Station of the Warsaw University, and the Mammal Research Institute of the Polish Academy of Sciences.

In 1977, Białowieża National Park was recognised as a UNESCO Man and Biosphere Reserve, being a typical example of the European mixed deciduous forests of the boreo-nemoral zone. Two years later, Białowieża National Park, as a forest with "outstanding universal value", unique on a global scale, received the status of a UNESCO World Heritage Site. In 1996, as a result of a national and international campaign addressed to the Polish government, the size of the Białowieża National Park was doubled to cover 100 km^2 (Figure 2.1). In 2003, Białowieża village, with about 2,000 permanent residents, was visited by over 120,000 tourists.

During the first post-war decades, the area of the Białowieża Forest managed by the State Forests in the three forest districts of Białowieża, Browsk and Hajnówka underwent notable changes in

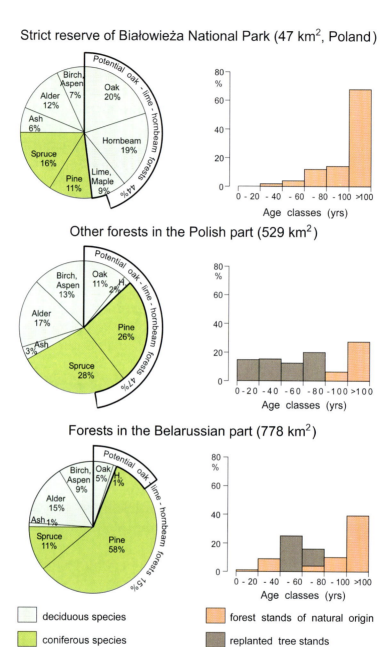

Figure 2.2. Species and age structure of tree stands in the three parts of Białowieża Forest that differ in management rules: strict reserve of Białowieża National Park (pristine forests), other forests in the Polish part (exploited for timber with varying intensity since 1915 and partly protected in some sections since the 1970's), and forests in the Belarussian part (exploited for timber in 1915–1941, and protected by varying regimes afterwards). The graphs represent the situation in the early 1990's. (Reprinted from: *Predation in vertebrate communities.* Springer Verlag, Berlin, 1998; modified.)

species and age structure due to clear-cutting and replantation (Figure 2.2). For a long time, only 1–3 species were preferred for replantations (mainly pine and spruce, later also oak). The secondary stands resembled typical European monocultures of trees rather than primeval forests. Fortunately since the late 1970's, the management rules in Białowieża Forest have been changing towards more ecologically oriented forestry, with various forms of protection. In 2004, forest reserves in the Białowieża, Browsk and Hajnówka Districts covered a total of 115 km^2. However, some of the remaining old stands of natural origin are still left unprotected. Without doubt nature protection in Białowieża Primeval Forest needs to be improved.

Since 1945, the entire Belarussian section of Białowieża Forest, about 900 km^2 or 60% of the Forest's area, had been proclaimed as "*zapovednik*" (the highest rank of nature protection in the former Soviet Union, equivalent to strict reserve). However, in 1956 it became the Game Conservation Area Belovezhskaya Pushcha. The new management rules allowed for removal of dead wood from the forest, but logging of the living trees was still banned. In 1991, the independent Belarus Republic changed the status of the Forest into the National Park Belovezhskaya Pushcha. It covers the complete Belarussian section of Białowieża Forest and its outskirts, with a total area of 1650 km^2 in 2004, of which about 900 km^2 are actual woodstands of Białowieża Forest. The management rules of the National Park allow for modest exploitation of timber (so-called sanitary cutting), commercial hunts for game, including European bison, and control of wolves. In 1992, the Belarussian National Park also became a Man and Biosphere Reserve and a 51-km^2 section was included into a transboundary World Heritage Site.

Diversity of life

The great diversity of life in Białowieża Primeval Forest (Photo 2.2) stems from its geographic location (see Chapter 3) and the large portion of well-preserved forests of natural origin. The local climate is under strong continental influence, with dry hot summers and cold, snowy winters. The mean annual temperature for the last 50-year period averaged 7.0°C, and the mean annual precipitation was 620 mm. The vegetative season is relatively short, on average 208 days with a mean daily temperature >5°C, which precludes the occurrence of the West European (Atlantic) tree species, such as beech or sycamore.

The most common forest association of Białowieża woodlands is the oak-lime-hornbeam forest (Photo 2.1). Oak and lime, with admixtures of spruce and maple, form the upper canopy layer. The lower layers are dominated by hornbeam and young limes. Typical of this forest type is the mass blossoming of flowers in spring, before the leaves develop. Later, in summer, canopy coverage reaches 70–90%. Natural regeneration is usually taking place in small gaps created by single dying or windfallen trees. In oak-lime-hornbeam forest, growing on rich brown and grey-brown podzolic soils, trees attain very large dimensions and long lifespans – oaks may grow to 2 metres of diameter at breast height and over 500 years of age. The tallest trees are spruces, reaching up to 55 metres.

Wet areas are covered by bog alderwoods (areas of stagnated water) and ash-alder forests on the flooded plains alongside the forest's rivers (Photo 2.1). Black alder with admixtures of birch, spruce, and rowan form the first association, whereas the latter is built of ash, alder, elm, and bird cherry. Rich in water for most of the year, these forest types are essential habitats for the amphibians: common and moor frogs, tree frogs, and common toads. Many of the

Photo 2.2. Natural, old-growth forests of Białowieża are characterised by a great diversity of life. Photos by Paweł Fabijański.

floodplain valleys in Białowieża Forest have been cleared and utilised as riverside meadows from as early as the 16th century. These meadows, 0.1–2 km wide, and covered in sedges and grasses (see Chapters 14 and 17), had been scythed and grazed by cattle until the mid 20th century in the Polish part of the Forest and are still being utilised in the Belarussian section.

Dry, sandy soils are covered with coniferous, pine-spruce forests (Photo 2.1). Birch and aspen form stands with conifers, and the ground is covered by a thick layer of dwarf shrubs, ferns, and mosses. In the past centuries, frequent ground fires caused by people controlled the spruce and promoted pine regeneration. With effective fire prevention in the 20th century, the role of spruce in coniferous forests increased.

A very characteristic feature of Białowieża Forest is the natural sequence of forest associations, determined by water regimes and soil types (Figure 2.3). Furthermore, besides the main associations, the rich natural forests have many transitional forms and endless, small-scale patch diversity. Regardless of the forest type however, the old-growth stands are characterised by two important features: the abundance of dead wood in various stages of decay, and the presence of numerous species defined as relics of natural forests. These include species of fungi, lichen, plants, invertebrates and vertebrates that in the past had occurred in temperate and boreal forests across Europe. However, with large-scale deforestation and transformation

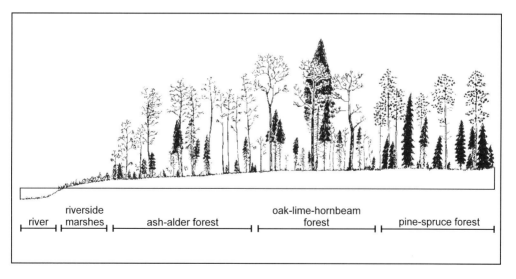

Figure 2.3. Topographic sequence of the natural non-forest and forest communities in Białowieża Forest, in the terrain profile from the river valley to the local watershed. Drawing by Tomasz Samojlik.

of the remaining woodlands into commercial monocultures, many of these species disappeared or exist on the edge of extinction. Most of the relic species are dependent on undisturbed old stands or dead wood.

Białowieża Forest still harbours a great diversity of life. For example, its fauna currently includes over 12,000 species, but specialists estimate that we may only know about 50% of the actual number of species living in the Forest. The best way to preserve this enormous biodiversity is to protect natural habitats and ecological processes. We must find an alternative to commercial use of large parts of the Forest, but on the other hand we also need to avoid disturbance caused by the massive increase in tourism. Only wise, balanced management and protection rules, based on a deep respect for the natural and cultural values of Białowieża Forest will allow this legacy from our ancestors to be passed on to future generations in as good a shape as possible.

Suggested readings

Bobiec A. 2002. Living stands and dead wood in the Białowieża Forest: Suggestions for restoration management. Forest Ecology and Management 165: 121–136.

Faliński J. B. 1986. Vegetation dynamics in temperate lowland primeval forests. Dr W. Junk Publishers, Dordrecht: 1–537.

Gutowski J. M. and Jaroszewicz B. (eds) 2001. Catalogue of the fauna of Białowieża Primeval Forest. Instytut Badawczy Leśnictwa, Warszawa: 1–403.

Tomiałojć L. 1991. Characteristics of old growth in the Białowieża Forest, Poland. Natural Areas Journal 11(1): 7–18.

3

Biodiversity of forest mammals

**Krystyna Stachura, Magdalena Niedziałkowska
and Kamil Bartoń**

Why does Białowieża Primeval Forest, a woodland of 1500 km², harbour as many as 57 mammal species? Firstly, it is one of the last pristine woodlands in temperate Europe. Secondly, it is located in a rare junction of the continent, where faunal elements from North and South, East and West meet and coexist.

All bison's friends and relations

Although Białowieża Primeval Forest is famous for large animals such as the European bison, wolf and lynx, the most diverse groups of mammals are rodents (18 species), bats (12 species) and predators (12 species). The woodlands of Białowieża also harbour 8 species of insectivores, 2 lagomorphs, and 5 ungulates. In total, the mammalian community consists of 57 species living in natural environments of forests and river-side marshes, and within small glades in traditional villages located in Białowieża Forest (Table 3.1).

The community of forest rodents is dominated by bank voles and yellow-necked mice, which also play an essential ecological role by supporting several species of vertebrate predators: carnivores and birds of prey (see Chapter 16). All the rodent species are herbivores in a broad sense, though they may supplement their diets with invertebrates, mainly in spring and summer. Apart from common and well-studied species, a few rare, arboreal rodents inhabit the old growth forests. These are the fat dormouse (Photo 3.1), common

Table 3.1. Mammalian species recorded in the woodlands, marshy river valleys, and glades within human settlements in the range of the Białowieża Primeval Forest. For most taxa, percentage shares in the respective forest--dwelling communities are calculated based on numbers and biomass. Dominant and subdominant species (percentage share > 5%) are in bold. Some species were not included into calculations due to the fact that they either inhabit largely non-forest habitats, or there are no data available on their densities. Conservation status in Poland and Europe was based on: the IUCN Red List of Threatened Animals & European Verterbrate Red Data Book (CR – Critically endangered, EN – Endangered, Vu – Vulnerable, LR-nt – Lower Risk – near threatened, LR-cd – lower risk-conservation dependent, LR-lc – lower risk-least concern) and the Polish Red Data Book of Animals (as above, plus: NT – Near Threatened, LC – Least Concern). P – species protected.

Species	Share in community (%)		Conservation status	
	Numbers	Total biomass	Poland	Europe (IUCN)
Rodents				
Bank vole	**53.1**	**43.9**		
Yellow-necked mouse	**26.0**	**39.2**		
Pine vole	**7.0**	**5.8**		
Northern birch mouse	4.5	1.7	P	LR-nt
Field vole	4.3	4.8		
Root vole	1.8	2.3		LR-nt
Harvest mouse	1.2	0.5		LR-nt
Common vole	1.1	1.0		
Striped field mouse	1.0	0.8		
Wood mouse				
Water vole				
Beaver			P	LR-nt
Red squirrel			P	LR-nt
Fat dormouse			P, NT	LR-nt
Common dormouse			P	LR-nt
Forest dormouse			P, NT	LR-nt
Brown rat				
Eastern house mouse				
Lagomorphs				
Brown hare				
Mountain hare			P, EN	
Bats				
Noctule	**29.4**	**57.1**	P	
Daubenton's bat	**22.3**	8.7	P	
Leisler's bat	**15.9**	**15.4**	P, Vu	LR-nt
Nathusius' pipistrelle	**8.5**	3.8	P	
Parti-coloured bat	**6.9**	**6.2**	P, LC	
Common pipistrelle*	**5.3**	2.1	P	

continued on the next page

Table 3.1. continued.

Species				
Northern bat	4.0	2.6	P, NT	
Barbastelle	2.4	1.6	P	VU
Brown long-eared bat	2.4	1.2	P	
Natterer's bat	2.0	1.0	P	
Brandt's bat	0.9	0.3	P	
Serotine			P	
Insectivores				
Common shrew	**72.0**	**74.1**	P	
Pygmy shrew	**16.0**	**7.2**	P	
Water shrew	**8.0**	**14.4**	P	
Mediterranean water shrew	3.0	3.7	P, LC	
Masked shrew	1.0	0.6	P, NT	
Bi-coloured white-toothed shrew			P	
Eastern hedgehog			P	
Common mole			P	
Ungulates				
Red deer	**38.3**	**46.4**		
Roe deer	**31.6**	**7.6**		
Wild boar	**25.0**	**24.2**		
European bison	3.8	**18.5**	P, EN	EN
Moose	1.3	3.3		
Carnivores				
Weasel	**52.4**	2.7	P	
Pine marten	**16.2**	**12.2**		
Polecat	**12.4**	**6.5**		
Stoat	**5.7**	1.0	P	
Raccoon dog	4.8	**20.7**		
Lynx	1.2	**15.9**	P, NT	
Wolf	0.7	**15.1**	P, NT	VU (Italy); LR-cd (Portugal and Spain)
Red fox	2.8	**12.1**		
American mink	1.9	1.1		
Badger	1.0	**9.7**		
Otter	0.9	3.0	P	
Stone marten				
European mink	extinct**		Ex	EN
Brown bear	extinct**		NT	LR-lc

* a newly recognised species, *Pipistrellus pygmaeus*, was distinguished from the common pipistrelle *P. pipistrellus*, based on different frequencies of emitted signals. Probably in Białowieża Forest, all individuals reported earlier as common pipistrelles belong to the new species *Pipistrellus pygmaeus*.
** extinct from Białowieża Forest.
(Data on community structures from: *Predation in vertebrate communities*. Springer Verlag, Berlin, 1998.)

dormouse, and forest dormouse. Their secretive, nocturnal life style and long period of winter hibernation place them among the least understood animals of Białowieża Forest. The biggest European rodent, the beaver, inhabits the rivers of the region. A true engineer of aquatic habitats, the beaver is a key-species with ecological importance reaching beyond its mere numbers or biomass in the mammalian community.

Open terrain occupies less than 10% of the Białowieża Forest, consisting of river-side marshes overgrown with sedges and reeds, and settlement glades of field and meadows. Root voles dominate in wet marshy habitats, and common voles in drier, agricultural land and pastures. Stripes of narrow (0.1–2 km) open marshes in river valleys used to be home to water voles. However, the species has declined heavily during the last 20 years after the marshes have been colonized by the American mink.

Terrestrial insectivorous mammals occupy the same wide range of habitats as rodents do, but they have specialised in hunting invertebrates. The smallest mammal of Białowieża Forest, the pygmy shrew (adult body mass 3.5 grams), belongs to this group. The forest guild of small insectivores is strongly dominated by common shrews (Table 3.1) but in the immediate vicinity of streams they are outnumbered by water shrews, the semiaquatic species (see Chapter 19).

Photo 3.1. The fat dormouse, a rare arboreal rodent typical of mature forests. Photo by Sławomir Wąsik.

Bats are among the least known mammals of Białowieża Forest. They are very difficult to investigate due to their nocturnal activity, seasonal migration, and preference for living in cavities located high up in the trees (see Chapter 15). Some species of bats can only be distinguished from others by the frequency of their emitted sounds. An example would be the common pipistrelle and a new species *Pipistrellus pygmaeus*. The most numerous bats in Białowieża Forest are the common noctule and the Daubenton's bat. Together they make up more than 50% of bat numbers and above 60% of their total biomass (Table 3.1). The serotine bat occurs only in human settlements located in the forest.

The Białowieża ungulate community is one of the richest in temperate Europe. It includes the European bison, the largest terrestrial mammal of the remaining European fauna. The bison is one of the rarest species by numbers, though it contributes a considerable biomass. The wild boar, which roots through the soil in search of food, is important for soil turnover and for the reproduction of some plant species. The dominant ungulate species by both abundance and biomass is the red deer (Table 3.1).

The predator community became impoverished in the 19th and early 20th centuries by the extinction of the European mink and brown bear (see Chapter 9). Nowadays, 12 species of carnivores, ten native and two introduced, the American mink and the raccoon dog, can be found in Białowieża. The dominant species by numbers is the weasel (52% of the community) but due to its small size, it contributes

Table 3.2. Shannon-Wiener diversity (H) and equitability (H/H_{max}) indices of the mammalian communities in Białowieża Forest, calculated for: N – percentage share of individuals by numbers, Bm – percentage of total biomass. Communities with the highest equitability index have the most even allotment of individuals among the species.

Group	Number of species		H		H/H_{max}	
	Total	Used for calculations	N	Bm	N	Bm
Rodents	18	9	1.98	1.89	0.59	0.60
Lagomorphs	2	–	–	–	–	–
Bats	12	11	2.83	2.13	0.82	0.62
Insectivores	8	5	1.27	1.22	0.55	0.52
Ungulates	5	5	1.82	2.27	0.78	0.98
Carnivores	12	11	2.24	3.05	0.65	0.88
Total	57					

only 2.6% to the carnivore biomass. In terms of biomass, the most important species in the community is the raccoon dog. The largest species in the community, the wolf and the lynx, together make up about 30% of carnivore biomass (Table 3.1).

Based on Shannon-Wiener indices of diversity and equitability (Table 3.2), we can conclude that bats and ungulates are the most diverse group of mammals, with the most regular share of each species in the community. The least varied – strongly dominated by 1–2 species – are insectivores and rodents. Among all mammals inhabiting the Białowieża Forest, 33 species are protected by law in Poland. Among them are 12 species recorded in the Polish Red Data Book of Animals and 14 species in the IUCN Red List of Threatened Species (Table 3.1).

Geographical ranges of Białowieża mammals

Due to its location close to the geographical center of Europe, Białowieża Forest is a meeting point for most of the major faunal elements present on our continent. These include typical boreal, temperate and southern species as well as those with a range covering two or more zones (Figure 3.1).

Among the mammals of Białowieża Forest, there are only two truly boreal species with their main distribution in tundra and taiga: the mountain hare and the masked shrew (Table 3.3). Both are regarded as postglacial relics. The mountain hare reaches its south-western limit here, while Białowieża Forest is the only place where the masked shrew occurs in Poland. Moreover, the isolated population in the Forest is located far beyond the southern limit of the contiguous range of this shrew species.

The boreo-temperate group contains species found equally in the boreal and the temperate zone. There are 16 such species in Białowieża Forest (Table 3.3). Some boreo-temperate species might exceed the said range, for instance the otter is also found in the Mediterranean basin and in some parts of the Oriental region. This group also includes species, such as the beaver and the lynx, that were once widely distributed over European woodlands, but due to hunting and habitat loss they disappeared from vast areas of Western Europe (see Chapter 11). Some of the more numerous rodents (bank vole), insectivores (common shrew, pygmy shrew), and bats (Daubenton's bat), which are dominant or co-dominant in their respective mammalian communities, belong to the boreo-temperate faunal group.

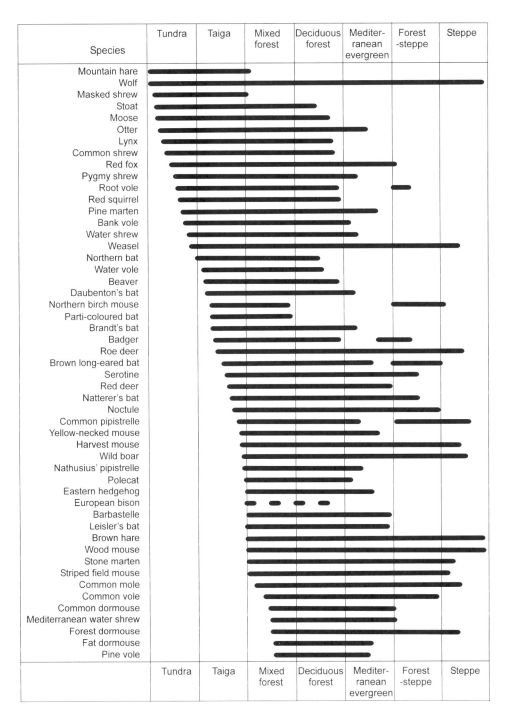

Figure 3.1. Schematic span of the geographical ranges of Białowieża Forest's mammals in the European biomes. 51 native species, occurring predominantly in woodlands are shown out of a total number of 57 recorded species. Broken line – original historical range of the European bison (see Chapter 4).

Mammals in the broad temperate group are distributed mainly in the temperate zone, but may occur in the boreal and southern zone. One representative of this group is the roe deer, which has the widest range in Europe, reaching the Polar Circle in the north and the Balkan Peninsula in the south (Figure 3.1). Although in Asia its range narrows, the roe deer can still be found between the southern border of taiga and the northern border of the temperate desert zone. Another example is the wild boar. Primarily an inhabitant of temperate broadleaved forest in Europe or tropical monsoon forest in Asia, wild boar is extending its range into other biomes. This group contains also strictly temperate species, with geographic ranges restricted to European broadleaved and mixed forests. Some of those mammals are European endemics. The most outstanding representative is the European bison. Another example is the polecat. Generally, the broad temperate group comprises 16 species, or 28% of the mammalian fauna of Białowieża Forest (Table 3.3). Again, several of them are quite numerous or even dominating species, e.g.

Table 3.3. Frequency distribution of the mammalian species inhabiting Białowieża Forest in the zoogeographic faunal groups.

Faunal group	Description of the species' range	Number of species	Percentage of total number of species
Boreal	Species with main distributions in tundra and taiga zones	2	3.5
Boreo-temperate	Species which occur equally in boreal and temperate forest zones	16	28
Broad temperate	Species with main distributions in the temperate forest zone, but occurring also in parts of the neighbouring zones	16	28
Southern temperate	Species found in temperate woodlands and south of the temperate forest zone	12	21
Holarctic	Species which occur widely in Eurasia and North America	7	12.5
Introduced	–	2	3.5
Synanthropic	–	2	3.5
Total		57	100

the noctule in the bat community and the yellow-necked mouse among the forest rodents.

The southern temperate group includes species that are found across the temperate forest zone and in the more southern regions. This group can be subdivided into temperate-Mediterranean and temperate-continental groups. Interestingly, these groups are represented by three species of rare arboreal dormice and yet another European endemic species, the Mediterranean water shrew. Southern temperate species form 21% of the local mammalian fauna. Białowieża Forest is often on (or near) the northern border of their geographical ranges.

There are seven Holarctic species, which occur widely in Eurasia and North America. Among them the red fox (Photo 3.2), the weasel and originally the wolf have outstandingly large geographical ranges. Red deer inhabit temperate woodlands and moose typically dwell in the boreal forest zone.

Białowieża Forest is inhabited by two non-native species of carnivores. The American mink from the Nearctic and the raccoon dog from the Oriental realm were introduced to the European part of the former Soviet Union in the 1920's–1950's, and they colonised Central and Eastern European countries. Two synanthropic species, the house mouse, and the brown rat have accompanied humans from the early days of civilization. They are commonly recorded in villages and settlements located in Białowieża Forest.

Photo 3.2. Juvenile red foxes. The red fox is one of the most widely spread mammal in the world. Photo by Sławomir Wąsik.

Local habitat preference of mammals

In addition to the geographical gradient of boreal forest, temperate woodlands and southern steppe, the local biotopes also vary from poor coniferous forest to rich, multispecies deciduous stands, and to open areas, largely created by human activity. These habitats influence the distribution of mammals mainly through changes in food supply and availability of shelters. Habitat preferences of mammals in Białowieża Forest are shown here for two groups of species, carnivores (Figure 3.2) and small terrestrial rodents (Figure 3.3).

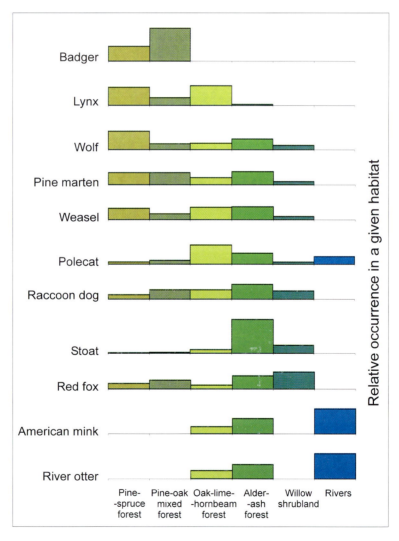

Figure 3.2. Habitat preferences of 11 species of carnivores co-existing in Białowieża Forest. (Based on data from: *Predation in vertebrate communities*. Springer Verlag, Berlin, 1998.)

Oak-lime-hornbeam and alder-ash forests are typical forest associations of temperate deciduous woodlands in Central Europe. They grow on rich soils and form dense canopies. These habitats provide the most favourable conditions for many small mammals including the yellow-necked mouse, bank vole, pine vole, and northern birch mouse. Predators that prefer deciduous forests include badgers (see Chapter 12) and polecats. Coniferous, pine-spruce forests grow on dry, sandy soils. This type of habitat is not particularly preferred by mammals, but several species, such as lynx, wolf and weasel, may select a mosaic of coniferous and wet deciduous forests. Meadows and sedge and reed marshes are the most important non-forested biotopes in Białowieża Forest. Mammals inhabiting these environments include the stoat, American mink, and otter, as well as the water vole and root vole (see Chapter 17).

At both national and European scales, Białowieża Primeval Forest is an important refuge for mammals, including common and threatened species. The best way to preserve this unique biodiversity is to protect the animals' natural habitats.

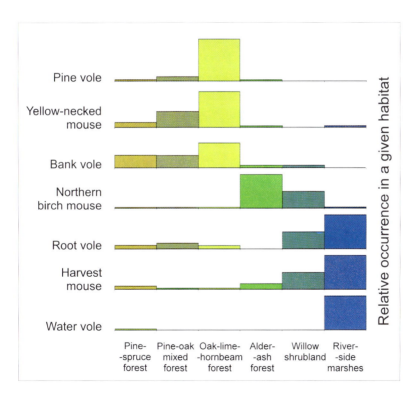

Figure 3.3. Habitat preferences of seven species of rodents inhabiting woodlands and marshy river valleys in Białowieża Forest. (Based on data from: *Acta Theriologica* 15: 465–515, 1970.)

Suggested readings

Aulak W. 1970. Small mammal communities of the Białowieża National Park. Acta Theriologica 15: 465–515.

Głowaciński Z. (ed.) 2001. Polish Red Data Book of Animals. Vertebrates. Państwowe Wydawnictwo Rolne i Leśne, Warszawa.

Jędrzejewska B. and Jędrzejewski W. 1998. Predation in vertebrate communities. The Białowieża Primeval Forest as a case study. Springer Verlag, Berlin: 1–450.

Macdonald D. W. and Barret P. 2001. Mammals of Europe. Princeton: 1–312.

Mitchell-Jones A. J., Amori G., Bogdanowicz W., Krystufek B., Reijnders P. J. H., Spitzenberger F., Stubbe M., Thissen J. B. M., Vohralik V. and Zima J. 1999. The atlas of European mammals. T & AD Poyser Natural History: 1–484.

Pucek Z. (ed.) 1981. Keys to verterbrate of Poland. Mammals. Państwowe Wydawnictwo Naukowe, Warszawa.

Wallace A. R. 1876. The geographical distribution of animals. Vols 1–2. Harper & Brothers, New York.

4

European bison
– history of a flagship species

Zdzisław Pucek

At one time, the European bison, the largest terrestrial mammal of Europe, was widely distributed throughout our Continent. However, habitat degradation and fragmentation, unlimited hunting and poaching, were the main factors leading to a decrease in population numbers and eventual extinction in the wild. One of the last refuges of the European bison was the Białowieża Primeval Forest, where they survived until 1919. It was also here, immediately after World War I, that the first efforts were made to save this species.

Extinction of the species in the wild

In historical times the range of European bison covered Western, Central and Southeastern Europe. Shrinkage and fragmentation of their range, as well as decreasing numbers and increased isolation of sub-populations led to their extinction (Figure 4.1). From the fragmentary information chronicled, we can estimate that bison in Gallia were the first to die out in the 8th century. In the south of Sweden they survived until the 11th century. In northeast France, the existence of European bison was reported until the 14th century. In Brandenburg, they were already kept and bred in enclosures by the 16th century. In eastern Prussia, however, bison survived a relatively long time; in 1726, their numbers were estimated at 117 individuals, but in 1755 the last two animals were killed by poachers between Labiau (today Polesk) and Tilsit (today Sovetsk). In the 16th century,

European bison became extinct in Hungary, although some animals survived for a long period in Transylvania, with the last individual being poached in 1790. In Romania, the last European bison was killed in the Radnai Mountains in 1762. In Eastern Europe, bison existed until the 17th and 18th century along the River Don (1709) and in Moldova (1717). The last free ranging population survived in the Caucasus Mountains until 1927.

In Poland, by the 11th and 12th centuries, the European bison populations were limited to the larger forest complexes, where they were protected as the royal game. In the 15th century Polish--Lithuanian Commonwealth, they were found in Niepołomicka Forest, Sandomierska Forest, Białowieża Forest, near Ratna on the Pripet River and in Volhynia. In the Kurpiowska Forest, they became extinct in the 18th century. One the first legal acts concerning the protection of European bison, as well as auroch, beaver, and other animals, were the so-called "Lithuanian Statutes", declared by King Sigismund the Old in 1532.

Favourable circumstances enabled European bison to survive until 1919 in Białowieża Primeval Forest (Figure 4.2). Since the 14th century, this well-preserved lowland forest was under special protection as the property of Lithuanian Dukes, Polish kings, and during the period of partition of Poland (1795–1915), of Russian czars. In the 19th century, the population of bison in Białowieża Forest

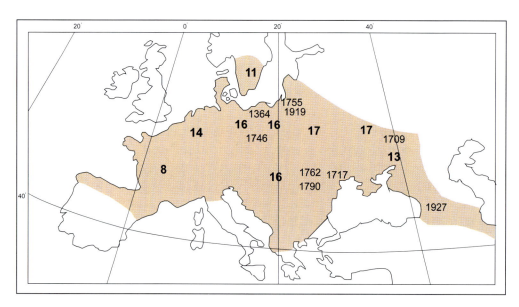

Figure 4.1. Reconstructed range of the European bison in Holocene and early historical times (coloured area). Century (in bold) and year of last bison records are shown in the given part of the range.

numbered about 500 to 800 individuals, although in short periods a minimum of 200 and a maximum of 1898 heads were recorded (Figure 4.3). Since 1888, the forest became the Czar's hunting ground. During this time the forest was overstocked with big game (especially deer) as well as cattle pastured in the woods. Both these factors impoverished the natural food resources for bison.

A slump in the population of European bison and other herbivores occurred during World War I. German divisions entered the Białowieża Forest in August 1915, and killed a large numbers of animals to supplement the army's lack of supplies. Although the German administration introduced hunting laws on the 25th September 1915, which provided punishment for killing bison, this species was still poached and their numbers decreased rapidly. A population count in January

Figure 4.2. Male and female European bison from Białowieża Forest. This drawing by Jan Piwarski, one of the first illustrations of European bison in the Polish literature, was first published in 1830 in a book by Feliks P. Jarocki, a zoologist from Warsaw University.

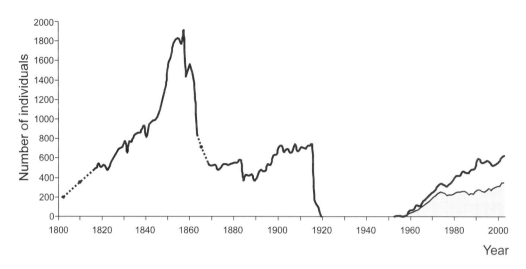

Figure 4.3. Population numbers of European bison in Białowieża Forest from the early 19th century until 2002. Shaded area denotes the number of individuals in the Polish part.

1916 revealed only 178 bison, and in March 1917, only 121 individuals were recorded (Figure 4.3). Temporary measures for their protection did not improve the situation, and by November 1918 there were only 68 European bison left. The German occupation of the forest continued until the end of 1918.

In the aftermath of World War I, chaos and the common abuse of law resulted in the last European bison being exterminated by poachers. In March 1919, the Polish authorities of the Ministry of Public Works and the Management of Eastern Territories sent Herman Knothe to Białowieża to organize the protection of European bison. Only a few bison tracks were found. During Knothe's second visit to the forest, the tracks of four bison and the remains of a poached individual were found on April 12, 1919. This was the last proven record of the European bison in Białowieża Forest

Restitution starts

The concept of saving the European bison, using animals kept in zoological gardens, was presented at the 1st International Congress of Nature Protection in Paris, on the 2nd of June, 1923, by the Polish naturalist, Jan Sztolcman. He appealed for the founding of an international organization whose task would be to save the bison. The Congress supported the appeal and by August 25–26, 1923, the International Society for Protection of European Bison (Internationale

Geselschaft zur Erhaltung des Wisents) was founded in Frankfurt on the Main. It included representatives from 16 countries and was chaired by K. Primel, the managing director of the zoological garden in Frankfurt. One important accomplishment during this early period of restitution was a thorough inventory of pure European bison. At that time, hybrids of European bison and North American bison, as well as with domestic cattle, were often bred in zoos. To distinguish pure European bison from these hybrids, a studbook known as the European Bison Pedigree Book (EBPB) was created. The first register reported 54 European bison with proven pedigrees. Of these, 39 originated from Białowieża. All crossbred bison were eventually eliminated from breeding with pure European bison due to the dedication and effort of the first editors of the EBPB. During the World War II another risky attempt to "increase the production" of European bison by crossing them with American bison was propagated by Nazi officials of the Third Reich in Schorfheide near Berlin. Fortunately, all these hybrids were eliminated from further restitution efforts. Erna Mohr (Germany) and Jan Żabiński (Poland) deserve special credit for twice rescuing the genetic purity of the world population of European bison by registering only pure blood animals to the EBPB. After World War II, the EBPB was edited in Poland under the auspices of the State Council of Nature Protection and more recently by Białowieża National Park.

During the recovery of the European bison, two periods can be distinguished. The first, lasting until 1952, involved the intensive breeding of bison in zoological gardens, parks, and specially created forest reserves designed for this purpose. In September and October 1929, the first four bison were brought from Warsaw Zoo to an enclosure in Białowieża Forest, these included the female Biscaya and bull Borusse. In 1936, the male Plish was brought from Pszczyna. In 1939, there were 16 bison in the reserve located in Białowieża Forest.

The second period of restitution began after 1952 and commenced with the creation of free-ranging herds, first in the Polish part of Białowieża Forest and later in the Belorussian part (Figure 4.3). In the Polish part, 38 bison were released until 1966, but only 28 took part in reproduction. In the Belorussian part, 43 animals, originating from Poland (Białowieża, Pszczyna) and Russia (Prioksko--terrasnyi Biosphere Reserve), were released into the wild between 1961 and 1967. In 2000, bison population roaming in Białowieża Forest reached the number of 571 individuals, including 306 individuals in the Polish part and 265 in the Belarussian part. So far, it remains the largest free-living population of European bison in the world.

One of the most important ideas, advocated in Poland during the initial recovery period of the European bison, was the distribution of the species over a large number of breeding centers. Progress in this area was recorded after World War II, when large confined herds in Poland and later also in the USSR produced founding animals for further reintroductions in the wild. Poland, and especially Białowieża Forest, played an important role in the global expansion of European bison. During the post-war period till 2000, 434 bison were transported from Białowieża to 11 countries.

The dynamics of the world population of European bison is illustrated in Figure 4.4. In the first period of restitution, the number of bison grew very slowly, with the rate of growth being seriously disturbed at the end of World War II. This was the second dramatic decrease of bison population in its recent history. In subsequent years, the population gradually increased. In places subject to war and civil unrest (e.g. the Caucasus), some small free-ranging herds have been exterminated or heavily poached. Finally, a number of animals are no longer registered in EBPB due to the lack of contact from particular breeders. This means that not all European bison are registered and the total world population of the species is estimated to be about a few hundred larger. The total number of European bison registered in EBPB in the world at the end of 2002 was estimated at approximately 3,070.

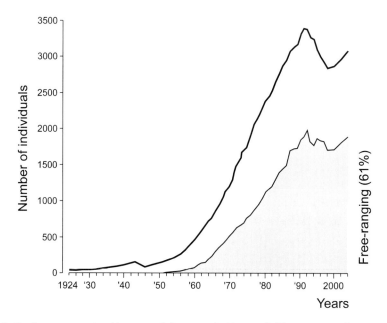

Figure 4.4. Increase in the world population of European bison. Shaded area denotes the free-ranging portion of the total population.

About 60% of the world population of European bison live in free and semi-free herds, distributed mainly within the historical range of the species (Figure 4.5). One of the aims of the European Bison Action Plan is to create a more compact geographic range for this species. The population of bison in Białowieża Forest, along with several others in north-east Poland, Lithuania, and Belarus, could be used for such a goal, especially if natural corridors were created to link them together as one metapopulation.

Threats and problems of management of European bison

The effects of restitution generally show a positive picture; however, a more critical insight into the current state of the species reveals serious threats stemming mainly from its genetic structure and from its management. The risk of extinction to the species remains high.

All purebred European bison are the descendants of 13 animals and represent a recombination of only 12 diploid sets of genes. Eleven founders originated directly or indirectly from Białowieża Forest. Two genetic lines are distinguished in the recent population of the species: the Lowland line (LB or Białowieża) originating from 7 founders (4 males, 3 females) and including pure animals of the *Bison bonasus bonasus* subspecies. One bull of *B. b. caucasicus*, born in 1907 in the Caucasus Mountains, was brought to Germany in 1908, and until his death in 1925, sired a number of calves from *B. b. bonasus* females, resulting in a separate line of purebred European bison called the Lowland-Caucasian line (LC). This last animal was the only influence of the Caucasian subspecies in the recovered species. Animals of both lines are carefully recorded in the EBPB and the principle of not merging these two lines is of particular importance for preserving the genetic variability of LC line.

The gene pool of European bison is limited and animals are highly inbred as a consequence of past bottlenecks. Inbreeding coefficients are very high compared to other large mammals averaging 44% in the Lowland line and 26% in the Lowland-Caucasian line. The negative effects of inbreeding, manifested in a decline in reproduction rate, are more strongly pronounced in the Lowland-Caucasian line than in the Lowland line. Inbreeding affects skeleton growth, particularly in females, and possibly lowers resistance to disease and pathologies.

The genetic contributions of the 12 founders to the contemporary world population of the European bison are highly dominated by one pair of animals. Some founders are not represented at all in particular free-ranging populations. There is evidence that genetic variability of the species has been declining, for instance due to reduction of genes represented by very rare founders. Furthermore, the second bottleneck in 1940–1945 caused that the founders' Y-chromosomes are not equally spread throughout the world stock of bison.

Another threat to European bison is the lack of space available for this large animal in contemporary ecosystems. Current populations are usually small, fragmented, and isolated each from the other (Figure 4.5). Furthermore, commercial forests are impoverished in terms of species composition and structure, and the goals of forestry administrations are often in conflict with the conditions required for the proper conservation of large browsers, such as European bison.

Diseases can potentially endanger bison populations. In Białowieża Forest, epizooties (e.g. foot and mouth disease) in bison were noted during the 19th century. Recently, the most important disease to arise is balanoposthitis, which results in the inflammation of the penis and prepuce, leading to diphteroid-necrotic lesions. Its origins and the effects on the reproduction and survival of the Białowieża population require further investigation.

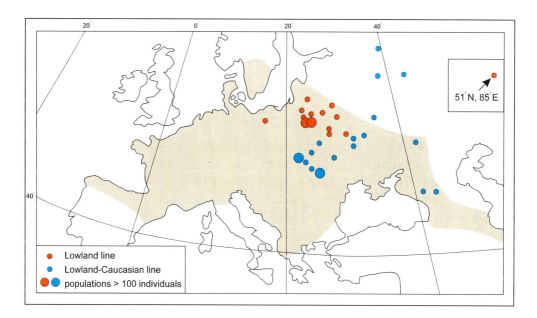

Figure 4.5. Contemporary (2002) distribution of free-ranging herds of the European bison. Red points – bison of Lowland line, blue points – bison of Lowland Caucasian line. Larger points indicate populations >100 individuals. Shaded area shows the original distribution of the European bison.

Management of free-ranging European bison populations, including that in Białowieża Forest (Photo 4.1), is based on practices typical for domestic animal husbandry rather than wildlife conservation and ecosystem ecology. Supplementary winter feeding reduces mortality, therefore the regulation of bison number does not depend upon natural factors but on the elimination of diseased, late-born, and aggressive animals by wildlife managers. To some extent, culling seeks to balance the population level. According to recent simulations for the bison population in Białowieża Forest, culling of adult females may heavily influence population growth.

European bison is an important element of ecosystem biodiversity in Białowieża Forest. Together with the other four large herbivores, moose, red deer, roe dear, and wild boar, it composes a rich community of mammals, unique in continental Europe. It can also be said that it is mainly due to the historic protection of European bison that the Białowieża Primeval Forest exists today, and attracts the attention of scientists and the admiration of Polish and foreign visitors.

Photo 4.1. Free-ranging European bison in Białowieża Forest. Photo by Jan Walencik.

Suggested readings

Jędrzejewska B., Jędrzejewski W., Bunevich A. N., Miłkowski L. and Krasiński Z. A. 1997. Factors shaping population densities and increase rates of ungulates in Białowieża Primeval Forest (Poland and Belarus) in the 19th and 20th centuries. Acta Theriologica 42: 399–451.

Krasiński Z. A. 1994. Restitution of the European bison in the Białowieża Reserve in years 1929–1952. Parki Narodowe i Rezerwaty Przyrody 4: 3–23. [In Polish with English summary]

Olech W. 1989. The participation of ancestral genes in the existing population of European bison. Acta Theriologica 34: 397–407.

Pucek Z. 1991. History of the European bison and problems of its protection and management. [In: Global trends in wildlife management. B. Bobek, K. Perzanowski and W. Regelin, eds]. Trans. 18th IUGB Congress, Kraków 1987. Świat Press, Kraków–Warszawa: 19–39.

Pucek Z., Seal U. S. and Miller P. S. [eds] 1996b. Population and habitat viability assessment for the European bison (*Bison bonasus*) IUCN/SSC Conservation Breeding Specialist Group. Apple Valley, Minnesota USA: 1–110.

Sztolcman J. 1924. Matériaux pour l'histoire naturelle et pour l'historique du Bison d'Europe (*Bison bonasus* Linn.). Annales zoologici Musei Polonici Historiae Naturalis 2: 49–136.

5

Life of the European bison

Małgorzata Krasińska and Zbigniew A. Krasiński

The European bison requires large, diverse complexes of deciduous and mixed forests in which to live. After many years in captivity, the species was finally returned to Białowieża Primeval Forest, the home of the last wild population before their extinction. Today, Europe's largest land mammal can be found wandering freely throughout the area; however, in order to survive a changing environment, this relict species should remain protected.

The annual life cycle of bison

When spring arrives in Białowieża Forest, around the middle of April, bison leave the places of winter supplementary feeding and begin to intensively forage on the fresh plant growth. They must make up for the deficiencies in their diet after the winter period (Figure 5.1). At this time, adult cows are in the final phases of pregnancy. The young will be born between May and July after approximately 9 months of pregnancy (264 days, on average). During the time of parturition, a cow leaves the herd, returning with her calf after a few days. Following the birth, the mother licks the calf, which is able to stand after 30 minutes and needs only another half an hour before attempting to suckle. The bond between mother and calf begins to weaken in the second month of life, and the young calves gather together more and more frequently. At the age of about 3 months their fur changes colour from a light brown to darker brown, resembling that of an adult bison.

The rutting season lasts from August to September and sometimes even till October (Figure 5.1). In mid-July, males over the age of 6 years begin to join the herds of cows and juveniles. During the rut, the bull accompanies the cow for 2–3 days. At this time, males demonstrate a number of typical sexual behaviours, which include emitting deep grunts. Sometimes conflicts arise between bulls which can result in fights where they push against each other with enormous strength (see Chapter 6).

Bison feed while moving. Fermentation processes occur continuously in the proventriculi, and especially in the huge rumen, the capacity of which exceeds 100 litres. Consequently, a regular food supply is required. Following rest during the night, bison resume feeding before sunrise, after which they lie down to ruminate the food. This cycle is repeated several times during the day. Between spring and autumn, bison spend approximately 60% of their daily activity feeding. Foraging on forest floor plants takes up 93% of feeding time, browsing 3%, and debarking 2%. Debarking occurs most intensively during the end of winter, in April, when it can even take up to 18% of feeding time. In winter, debarking is one method of obtaining natural food, and in other seasons it is a source of fibrous food necessary for normal digestion.

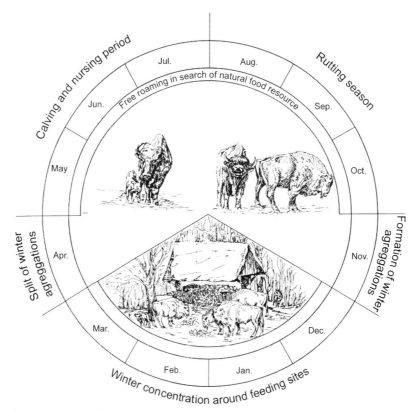

Figure 5.1. Annual life cycle of European bison.

The diet of the European bison includes 137 plant species, including 96 herbal plants, 27 trees and shrubs, and 14 grasses and sedge species. Among the herbaceous plants most frequently eaten are: goutweed, stinging nettle, buttercup, and garden thistle. Favourite grasses and sedges include reed grass, wood sedge and hairy sedge. Plants growing on the forest floor constitute up to 90% of the bison's food biomass, whereas food from trees (shoots and bark) is supplemental. Preferred trees and shrubs include goat willow, ash, and raspberry; the most commonly debarked trees are common oak, hornbeam, ash, and Norway spruce. In addition, acorns are a favourite food.

The vegetative season ends in November. Thus bison gather in large aggregations around the traditional supplementary feeding places. Cows with juveniles and calves are the first to gather, with adult bulls arriving later. During the winter, bison spend only 30% of their activity on feeding. When there is snow and frost, bison move very little (10% of their activity) to prevent unnecessary losses of energy. However, when the winter is mild and snow free, they wander throughout the forest searching for natural food sources. At the end of February, bison start to molt, beginning with the bulls, and then cows and juveniles. Towards the end of the winter, large mixed groups begin to split, and bison spread throughout the forest in search of the first green plants.

Herds and solitary individuals

The bison is a gregarious animal. During snow free periods, mixed groups and groups of bulls are the basic social units of the population. Mixed groups are formed by cows, juveniles (aged 2 to 3), calves, and occasionally adult bulls. The young stay with their mothers in the same group for up to 2 years. In the Polish part of Białowieża Forest, mixed groups consist of about 13 bison (Figure 5.2). In the Belarussian part, mixed groups are larger (averaging 21 individuals). In the Belarussian population, large groups can be encountered from August until October in mowed meadows and feeding glades. The size of mixed groups is seasonal, with the largest groups being formed during the rutting period (August and September).

Although bison groups are not formed according to family ties, it can be assumed that kinship does have an effect on the formation of large winter aggregations. Mixed groups originating from the same winter aggregations meet frequently, occasionally combine and then quickly split, exchanging some group members. The bonds between juveniles are least permanent, with young males exchanging groups frequently, whereas cows are the most stable. The leader of a mixed group is generally an older cow with a calf.

Young (1–2 years) males usually stay in mixed groups. Bulls aged 3–5 years are encountered in mixed groups as frequently as in separate groups of bulls. Young males, up to 6 years, form small groups of 2 to 8 individuals. Adult bulls aged over 6 years wander solitarily or in pairs. Groups of bulls are less stable, and most commonly consist of 2 to 3 animals. Over half of all bulls live alone (Figure 5.2). The number of solitary bulls increases prior to the rut (in July), reaching 70–80% by August and September. These bulls wander in search of receptive cows.

In Białowieża Forest, bison gather around feeding sites during the winter (Photo 5.1). Within the Polish population, there are four

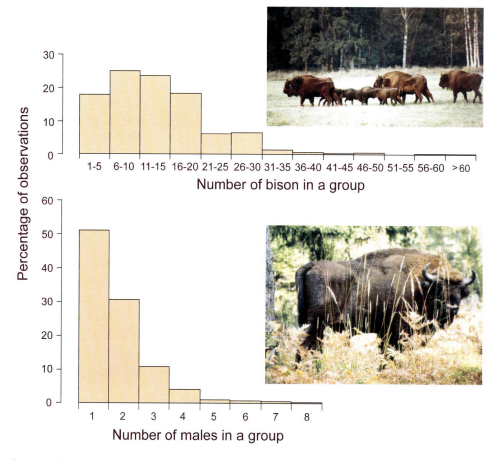

Figure 5.2. Frequency distributions of the size of mixed groups (upper graph) and bull groups (lower graph) in the population of the European bison in Białowieża Forest. Photos by Zbigniew A. Krasiński.

winter aggregations: two smaller ones (10–45 bison) and two larger ones, which are more stable (45–125 bison). Only one-third of adult bulls join winter aggregations, whereas others form separate bulls aggregations around feeding places or wander solitarily throughout the Forest (Photo 5.1).

Space needed to live

The bison is not a territorial animal but it requires a large area to live successfully Telemetry studies of radio-collared bison have provided data on the size of areas occupied by groups, as well as the home ranges of individuals. From spring to late autumn, the mean size of cow home ranges, and that of the mixed groups they belonged to,

Photo 5.1. In severe winters, cows with calves, juveniles, and some adult bulls concentrate around feeding sites, forming large aggregations (top). Some bulls spend winter in solitude and do not use supplementary food, instead penetrating the forest in search of natural foods (bottom). Photos by Zbigniew A. Krasiński.

was 69 km² (range 45–100 km²). This home range size for mixed groups was environmentally dependent. From August to October, large groups living in meadows and forest glades on the Belarussian side of the forest occupied ranges twice as small, as those of smaller groups inhabiting forests in the Polish part. Summer home ranges of mixed groups resulting from the break up of the different winter aggregations overlaped to a small degree (7%).

Bulls occupied home ranges of 29–152 km² (mean 70 km²). Bulls of a reproductive age (> 6 years) held much larger home ranges (mean 84 km²) than younger bulls. Bulls, located in the Forest periphery in the spring time, occupied the largest home ranges (136 and 152 km²) because they moved to areas occupied by cows in the breeding season. Home ranges of bulls and cows were found to overlap to a large extent.

Summer home ranges of bulls leaving the different winter aggregations were less spatially isolated from each other than those of mixed groups (16% overlapping). Home ranges of radio-collared cows

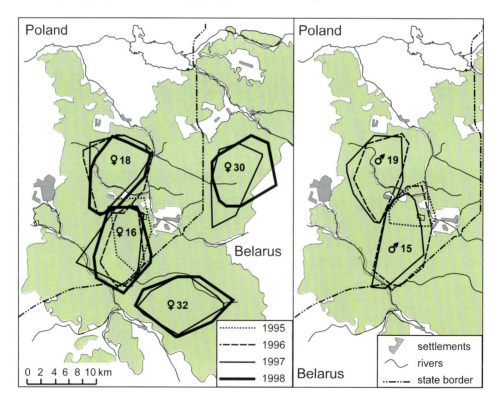

Figure 5.3. Radio-collared bison of both sexes (left: females, right: males), observed over several years, occupied spring-summer home ranges in the same parts of Białowieża Forest. (Reprinted from: *Acta Theriologica* 45: 321–334, 2000.)

and bulls, observed for several consecutive years, were situated in the same parts of the forest, overlapping 70–99% (Figure 5.3). This indicates high spatial fidelity of bison and home range stability.

In winter, bison concentrating around supplementary feeding sites occupied small home ranges (bulls 11 km^2 and cows 8 km^2, on average). However, the sizes of winter home ranges were significantly weather-dependent. During mild and snow free winters, bison occupied much larger home ranges (32–34 km^2). This indicates that low daily temperatures and long-term snow cover considerably limited bison mobility.

Extensive deciduous and mixed forests provide a natural environment for bison, ensuring an abundance of food throughout the vegetative season. In June and July, bison penetrate mixed coniferous forests more intensively. Alderwoods are exploited to a small extent, with their penetration by bison increasing in the summer during droughts. Open areas (mowed meadows, deforested feeding glades covered with grass, clearcuts and young plantations up to 10 years old), as well as forested areas, are utilised by bison.

Bison forage while moving and exhibit a specific feeding strategy (Figure 5.4). Herds move within the home range in search of food, led by an experienced cow, and never stay long in one place. Even when a herd of several dozen bison has passed through the area, traces left on the forest floor are indistinct. The strategy of environmental exploitation by bison is based on the size and structure of the group,

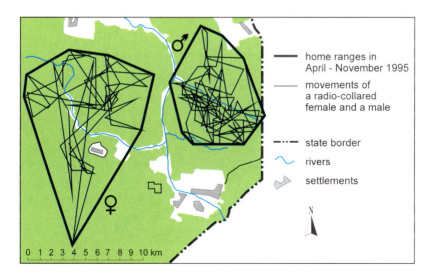

Figure 5.4. Movements and home ranges of radio-collared bison (a male and a female) during the snow free period of 1996. (Reprinted from: *Acta Theriologica* 45: 321–334, 2000.)

its biotope preferences, and rotational use of the area, thus preventing excessive use of forest floor vegetation.

The bison is a resident species, as lowland European bison have never been observed seasonally migrating. In Białowieża Forest, where bison density is relatively high (approximately 6 individuals/10 km^2), attempts to spread over the surrounding areas have been observed. In 1969, one bull passed to the Knyszyn Forest (30 km away). Temporarily (in early spring and autumn), single bulls, and groups of bulls and cows sometimes penetrate cultivated fields outside the Polish part of the forest, but they eventually return to the forest complex. In autumn of 2002, 3 cows appeared in the vicinity of Zbucz (10 km west of the Białowieża Forest), remaining there for the following winter and summer, giving birth and nursing their calves. In the same year, 3 bulls migrated to the Forest District of Żednia (15 km north of the Białowieża Forest).

The natural dispersal of European bison from Białowieża Forest to other forested areas in northeastern of Poland appears to herald a new stage in the conservation of this species. However, its future is also dependent upon positive changes in the landscape and ecologically friendly forest management.

Suggested readings

Borowski S. and Kossak S. 1972. The natural food preferences of the European bison in seasons free of snow cover. Acta Theriologica 17: 151–169.

Caboń-Raczyńska K., Krasińska M., Krasiński Z. A. and Wójcik J. M. 1987. Rhythm of daily activity and behavior of European bison in the Białowieża Forest in the period without snow cover. Acta Theriologica 32: 335–372.

Gębczyńska Z., Gębczyński M. and Martynowicz E. 1991. Food eaten by free-living European bison. Acta Theriologica 36: 307–313.

Krasińska M., Caboń-Raczyńska K. and Krasiński Z. A.1987. Strategy of habitat utilization by European bison in the Białowieża Forest. Acta Theriologica 32: 147–202.

Krasińska M. and Krasiński Z. A. 1995. Composition, group size, and spatial distribution of European bison bulls in Białowieża Forest. Acta Theriologica 40: 1–21

Krasińska M., Krasiński Z. A. and Bunevich A. N. 2000. Factors affecting the variability in home range size distribution in the Polish and Belarussian part of the Białowieża Forest. Acta Theriologica 45: 321–334.

Krasiński Z. A. 1978. Dynamics and structure of the European bison population in the Białowieża Primeval Forest. Acta Theriologica 23: 13–48.

6

Mating systems of ungulates

Katarzyna Daleszczyk

Four species of ruminants living in Białowieża Forest are polygamists. However, in each species males gain access to females in quite a different manner. There are territorialists, harem holders, and roving searchers among them.

Social and unsocial ungulates

European bison, moose, red deer, and roe deer are herbivorous ungulates. Besides notable differences in body size (from about 20 kg in roe deer to 400–900 kg in bison), the species are also characterized by different social systems (Figure 6.1), herd and home range sizes, and diets. The European bison is a social mammal. In winter, bison congregate in large herds of about 70–100 individuals in the vicinity of winter feeding places. From spring through autumn, they form two types of social units: the mixed groups and bull groups. The mixed groups, averaging 13 individuals, contain cows, calves and juveniles up to 3 years old. Adult males join these groups during the rutting season. Adult males (≥ 4 years of age) are either solitary or form small groups of 2–3 bulls. Mean annual home ranges of adult males and mixed groups are similar and cover 70–75 km^2 (see Chapter 5). The diet of European bison consists mainly of grasses, herbs and sedges (90% of rumen contents), supplemented by the bark and browse of trees and shrubs (10%).

The moose is the second largest ungulate in Białowieża Forest. Moose prefer a solitary life. During spring and summer in Białowieża Forest, males and non-reproducing females were seen alone, while breeding cows were accompanied by their calves. In winter, up to 4 moose could be observed together. Home ranges of non-migratory moose usually do not exceed 20 km^2 and are not defended. This species is generally a browser, with trees and shrubs constituting 90% of its diet.

The red deer is a gregarious species that is especially visible in winter, when 15% of groups number over 10 individuals. During spring and summer, males live alone or in small groups. Females form family units including one or several does with offspring from the current and previous year. Annual home ranges of stags (24 km^2)

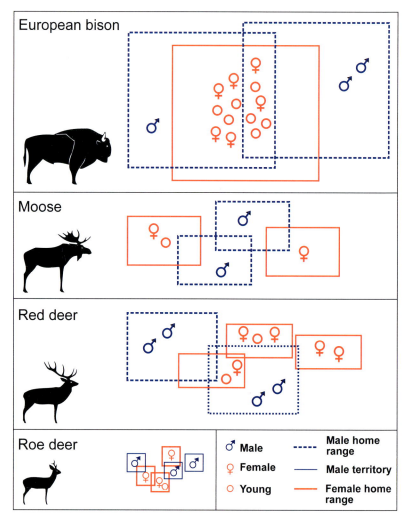

Figure 6.1. Schematic graph of social systems (herd size, home range or territory size and spatial distribution) in the four species of ruminants inhabiting Białowieża Forest.

are three times as large as the average female's range (8 km^2) (see Chapter 7). Shoots, bark, leaves and fruits of trees and shrubs, as well as dwarf shrubs form 60% of the red deer diet, while herbs, grasses and sedges constitute 40%.

The roe deer is rather an unsocial ungulate. Groups of up to 7 individuals were recorded in Białowieża Forest only in late autumn and winter. In spring and summer, males are solitary and females are found only with their own fawns. Male and female roe deer live in ranges comparable in size (from < 1 to several square kilometers), but from early spring males defend and mark their territories by rubbing their antlers and forehead against various objects, scraping the ground with their forehooves, and exhibiting aggression towards other males. One male territory may overlap ranges of several females and one female range may overlap with more than one male territory (Figure 6.1). After the rutting season, territorial behaviour of bucks ceases until the next spring. Roe deer forage on herbs, grasses, mosses, ferns, fungi and lichens (80% of annual diet) as well as on browse of trees and shrubs (20%).

Different faces of polygamy

Although all four species are polygamists, each has a different way of conducting reproductive activities (Figure 6.2). In polygynous species males have to compete for females. Competition may be displayed as defence of a territory, or defence of a group of females, or as rivalry for a high dominance rank while within a mixed herd.

For the moose, the rutting season takes place in September to October with the peak in the second half of September. In regards to its mating system, the moose belongs to roving males. Bulls roam the forest and utter calls while searching for cows. Sniffing the tracks, a bull finds a female in oestrus and stays with her for several days. During that stage, he leaves the cow only to fight an approaching rival. True fights are infrequent and most encounters are solved with displays. The quality of the male's call also provides information on his strength. When the cow's oestrus is over, the bull will search for another receptive female. Hence, during one rutting season the bull can form mating pairs with two or three consecutive females. During the mating season, moose display a peculiar behaviour of pawing out rut-pits. These shallow, elliptical pits are marked by males with urine. The first rut-pits are dug in the beginning of September. The function of rut-pits is unclear; probably they are marking places for males searching for a cow, or during encounters between bulls. In the rutting period, bulls roam more than in other seasons, spending more energy while foraging little, so they may lose about 10–15% of their weight.

The rutting season in red deer includes the second half of September and the first half of October. One of the first signs of an oncoming rut is the individual roaring of stags. In this period, male groups dissolve as bulls become intolerant of each other (Photo 6.1). The red deer is a harem breeder (Figure 6.2). Since hinds assemble in groups, the stags attempt to monopolise the entire group to mate subsequently with all adult females. Harem holders guard their females continuously, especially during the peak of the rutting season, and drive away all males that approach the harem. Males chased away from harems continue to circle, trying to mate with hinds foraging on the periphery.

Typical characteristics of the rutting season in red deer are roaring, male aggression and the strong smell of pheromones as males repeatedly sprinkle their bellies with urine. Stags can assess the strength of neighbouring males not only from their appearance but also from their scent and roaring. The roar, which is a com-

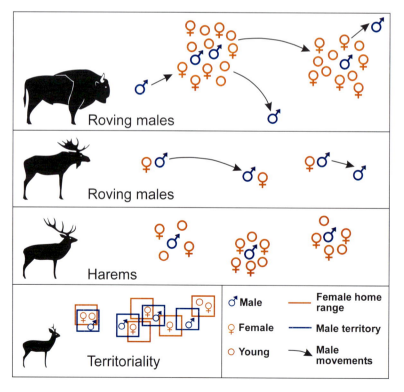

Figure 6.2. Schematic graph of the mating systems in four species of ruminants.

petitive display, can be heard at a long distance. Thus, the rivalry among red deer stags is – at least to some degree – carried out at a distance. Fights occur only if another stag wants to take over the harem. As such contests may be dangerous, stags assess their opponents carefully. True fights are usually limited to males 7–9 years old. The hierarchy among stags ceases with the casting of antlers. Similarly to the moose, a male red deer in rutting season may lose up to 15% of its weight.

In the roe deer, mating starts earlier, in the second half of July and lasts about one month. The most distinctive feature of the roe deer mating system is territoriality of males (Figure 6.2). Even before the onset of the rutting season, bucks become more mobile, penetrating their territories more intensively and "fighting" with shrubs and trees. Territoriality is connected with site-specific dominance: individuals win encounters on their ground, but they are losers on strange territories. A buck locates a female in oestrus by scent and follows her tracks. Sometimes the female may call to attract a buck's attention. The buck stays close to the female for a period of her oestrus, and after mating he leaves the female to search for another within his territory. When a female's range overlaps with more than one male's territory, she can move between them, being courted and mated by two or more territory holders. Some females also make rutting excursions outside their normal range to visit bucks with territories that do not overlap their range. Thus, it seems that female roe deer take an active role in mate searching.

Photo 6.1. Red deer stag in Białowieża Forest. Photo by Sławomir Wąsik.

Roving European bison

Moose, red deer, and roe deer are common in many areas while the presence of European bison is a rarity. Białowieża Forest is one of very few places, where this species lives in freedom and may be studied in its natural habitat. The rutting season for bison begins in the second half of July and ceases in October, with August and September being the strict rut. Males become sexually mature upon reaching 4 years old, although they are still growing up to the age of 6 years. As a result, these young mature males usually have no access to females in oestrus, as older and larger bulls can chase them away.

As the rutting season commences, bull groups break up and single males rove the forest searching for cows ready to mate (Figure 6.3). Seventy-eight percent of males seen outside mixed groups during this period are alone, in contrast to 47% solitary bulls in the pre-rut period. Walking from one mixed group to another, males increase their monthly home ranges considerably during the rut (Figure 6.3). Younger mature males already increase their spatial activity in July, while bulls of reproductive age expand their ranges only during the strict rut in August and September.

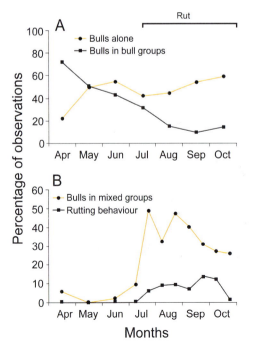
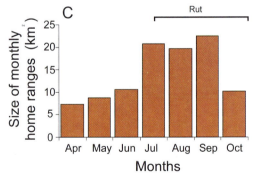

Figure 6.3. A. Changes in the structure of bull groups from April through October. B. Presence of bulls in the mixed groups and intensity of rutting behaviour (aggressive and sexual behaviours). C. Changes in the monthly home range size of European bison bulls from April through October.

Although there is no strict separation between sexes outside the mating season, bulls visit mixed groups considerably more often during the rut (Figure 6.3). Over 90% of mixed groups include adult males at this time, compared with only 22% outside the rut. In the rutting period, younger bulls were recorded in groups with cows twice as often as were the older males. During one rut, a mature male joins 5–6 mixed groups and spends, on average, 4 days in each. The younger the bull, the more groups he visits. It may be a way of increasing the possibility of gaining access to cows in oestrus.

During the rut, up to 4 adult bison males were seen in one mixed group at a time. When more than one bull is present in a group, a hierarchy is established among males and only the dominant bull will mate with the females. Males compete for a higher social rank using a variety of threats: pawing the ground with the forehooves, grunting (the vocalisation of bison), violent wallowing, scratching the ground or crashing shrubs with horns, uprooting smaller spruces, and chasing other males. Fights occur only when two bulls, similar in size and condition, want to rule the same mixed group (Photo 6.2). Contests last usually up to 15 minutes and consume a large amount of energy. The winner maintains his place in the group and hence the

Photo 6.2. European bison bulls fighting during the rutting season in Białowieża Forest. Photo by Zbigniew A. Krasiński.

access to receptive cows. The rutting behaviour of bison also includes sniffing of the cow's anogenital region. Flehmen or lip curl is commonly observed in bison. Lifting the upper lip while sniffing a female or her urine helps the male to check the composition of the scent and gain information about her readiness to mate. In bison, mating is preceded by characteristic courtship. A male and a female form the tending bond. A tending bull keeps himself close to the cow, parallel and a little behind, following her movements, occasionally trying to block them. Mock fights between the male and female as well as licking the female's sides, neck or rump may also take place. The bull repeatedly attempts to mount the cow but he usually fails to complete copulation until a day or two have passed. Tending usually lasts 1–3 days, after which the male looks for another mate.

So far, two main methods were used in researching the European bison mating system: radio-tracking and visual observations. Radio-tracking allowed collecting data on spatial activity of individuals, size of their home ranges, and length of distances walked. Visual observations provided information on changes in group structure, frequency in visiting females, and rutting behaviour. In the near future, population genetics methods (based on DNA analyses) will make it possible to study the reproductive success of various individuals as well as the degree of polygamy. Finally, it is worth mentioning that in many species of ungulates alternative mating strategies occur as a tool for less competitive males to also "get a piece of the cake". Accessibility of females, density of potential competitors, and other factors may modify the mating strategies of large herbivores.

Suggested readings

Clutton-Brock T. H. 1989. Mammalian mating systems. Proceedings of the Royal Society of London B 236: 339–372.

Dominey W. J. 1984. Alternative mating tactics and Evolutionary Stable Strategies. American Zoologist 24: 385–396.

Emlen T. and Oring L. W. 1977. Ecology, sexual selection, and the evolution of mating systems. Science 197 (4300): 215–223.

Krasiński Z. A., Krasińska M. and Bunevich A. N. 1999. Free-ranging populations of lowland European bison in the Białowieża Forest. Parki Narodowe i Rezerwaty Przyrody 18: 23–75.

7

Red deer – a tale of two deer

Jan F. Kamler, Bogumiła Jędrzejewska
and Stanisław Miścicki

Male and female red deer act so differently from each other, that many would believe them to be different species. Not only do stags and hinds have different home ranges, but they also have different activity patterns and sources of mortality. Because of their high numbers, feeding habits, and extensive movements, red deer help shape the forest community by influencing the regeneration of trees.

Movements in the forest

Red deer are the third largest herbivore in Białowieża Primeval Forest, smaller than bison and moose, but larger than roe deer and wild boar. However, red deer outnumber all other herbivores, and are an important food source for predators such as wolves and lynx. This suggests red deer are one of the most important herbivores in this natural forest ecosystem, possibly affecting the numbers and distributions of many plant and animal species.

Among all deer species, red deer are known for their strong sexual dimorphism, as males (stags) are almost twice as large as females (hinds). This large difference in body size usually affects red deer movements, as stags and hinds have different movement patterns in most areas of Europe. Red deer in Białowieża Forest are no exception, as they exhibit some of the greatest sexual differences in home ranges found in all of Europe (Figure 7.1). Radio-telemetry studies conducted in 2000–2004 revealed that hinds had annual

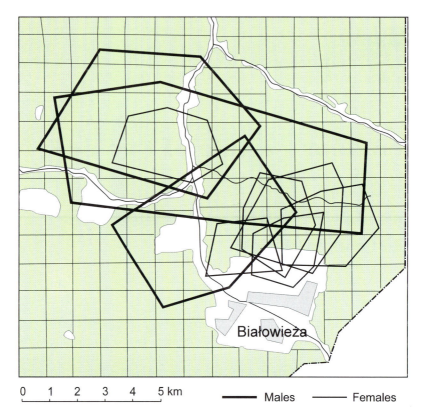

Figure 7.1. Home ranges of radio-tracked male and female red deer in Białowieża Forest, 2000–2003.

home ranges close to 8 km^2 (3 to 13 km^2), whereas home ranges of stags were 3-times larger at 24 km^2 (12 to 38 km^2).

Stags and hinds also show significant differences in seasonal home ranges. Hinds have mean home ranges of 2–4 km^2 during all seasons of the year. In contrast, stags have mean home ranges of 7–8 km^2 in winter and spring, but much larger ranges (13–14 km^2) in summer and autumn. There are several reasons for such differences. First, body size likely explains some of the variation as larger animals tend to have larger home ranges to meet their greater nutritional needs. However, body size alone is not a sufficient factor, as stags are only twice as large as hinds, yet stag home ranges are 3 to 7 times larger than those of hinds.

Differences in home ranges between sexes are probably most affected by their different reproductive strategies. Hinds rear young without assistance from stags (Photo 7.1), thus their reproductive success is most influenced by the abundance and distribution of food resources. In contrast, the reproductive success of stags is

Photo 7.1. A herd of female red deer. Photo by Sławomir Wąsik.

influenced most by access to multiple hinds, especially during the breeding season. This is why the stags increase their overall movements to obtain access to more hinds, and in consequence their home ranges increase dramatically during the breeding season (late summer and autumn).

Red deer in Białowieża Forest also show interesting differences in their daily ranges (ie. the area travelled in a 24-hr period). The mean daily ranges of hinds are 1–2 km^2 in all seasons, with the largest daily ranges in autumn. The mean daily ranges of stags are 1–1.5 km^2 in all seasons, with the smallest ones in autumn. Consequently, relative rates of home range use by stags and hinds differ most during autumn. During this season, females use 80% of their seasonal home range during a typical 24-hr period, whereas males only use 7%. This indicates that stags move a relatively short distance each day during autumn, although they move over much larger areas than hinds during that entire season. This interesting pattern probably results from stags following individual hinds on a daily basis during the breeding season (thus having small daily ranges), while constantly following different hinds in various areas throughout the entire breeding season (thus having much larger seasonal home ranges).

The daily, seasonal, and annual movements of red deer in Białowieża Forest are likely influenced by other factors as well. For example, red deer live in different sized herds throughout the year, yet the effect this has on their movement patterns is unknown. Other important factors are the presence of large predators, competition with other herbivores, breeding status, population density, and age. Compounded on top of all these factors is the fact that stags and hinds may be affected differently by each of these factors. Only by additional research will the importance of these other factors be better understood.

Activity patterns

Activity patterns are another important aspect of red deer ecology, as they explain "when" red deer move through the forest. In Białowieża Forest, the activity of radio-collared red deer was determined by obtaining locations at 15-minute intervals throughout a 24-hour period (Figure 7.2). There are two major aspects of red deer activity: circadian rhythm (ie. when they are active), and activity bouts (ie. duration of activity).

Similar to movement patterns, stags and hinds in BPF have different circadian rhythms. For example, during winter hinds are more active during the day than night, with peaks in activity just after sunrise, and again before dusk. In contrast, during winter stags

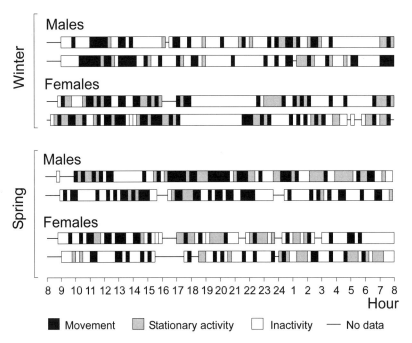

Figure 7.2. Activity patterns of radio-collared red deer, based on 24-h radio-tracking sessions with locations taken at 15-min intervals.

are active both day and night, with peaks in activity at midnight, and again at noon. Reasons for these differences in circadian rhythms are not clear. They might be related to herding behaviour, as hinds gather in much larger groups than stags during winter. Interestingly, circadian rhythms of wolves are similar to that of hinds, and most killings by wolves occur at dawn and dusk (see Chapter 10). This suggests that wolves adjust their activity to that of their main prey or vice versa (hinds must remain active when wolves are likely to be hunting).

The circadian rhythm of stags differs throughout the year. During both summer and autumn, when stags constantly search for hinds and have to guard groups of hinds from other stags, their activity and inactivity are distributed more uniformly throughout the day. In contrast, during winter and spring, when stags are solitary or in small groups, their circadian rhythm is more bimodal (which is the normal circadian rhythm of many large mammal species).

The typical daily activity of red deer in Białowieża Forest includes a sequence of numerous alternating bouts of activity and inactivity. In general, activity bouts are relatively short, lasting about 32 minutes in summer and autumn, and 43 minutes in winter and spring. Similarly, red deer have more activity bouts (on average, 22) in summer and autumn, than in winter and spring (17–18 bouts). Longer bouts of inactivity (>1.5 hours) are observed more often in winter and spring (11% of inactivity bouts) than in summer and autumn (1%).

These seasonal differences in the duration and frequency of activity bouts likely reflect changes in temperature. During winter, when temperatures in Białowieża Forest regularly reach −20°C, red deer rest for longer periods to conserve their energy. When red deer do become active during winter, they are active for longer periods, likely because they must increase feeding time as the amount and quality of forage declines.

Mortality

In most areas of Europe where wolves and lynx (the natural predators of red deer) have been extirpated, the primary cause of death in red deer populations is human hunting or starvation. Mortality can differ between stags and hinds, usually depending on the type of hunting permits allowed by local managers or landowners. Thus, the red deer population in Białowieża Forest offers a unique view of mortality patterns under more natural and evolutionary conditions.

As expected, wolves are the primary source of red deer mortality (see Chapter 10). Of 32 red deer that were radio-collared for research in 2000–2003, 8 were killed and eaten by wolves. Annual survival rate, ie. the chance of living for an entire year, was 62% for hinds and 86% for stags. Hinds have lower survival because wolves selectively prey more upon them than stags. Similarly, wolves selectively prey on much smaller juvenile red deer. Lynx are another major predator of red deer in Białowieża Forest (see Chapter 11), but they only prey upon smaller individuals such as hinds and juveniles.

In the whole Polish part of Białowieża Forest, red deer experience various pressures. In commercial forests (500 km^2), they have been hunted and may occasionally die in traffic accident on motorways. In the protected forests of the national park (100 km^2), no hunting and motor transportation is allowed. Large carnivores, disease, severe winter conditions, and possibly poachers operate in a similar way over the entire area. In the 1990's, the roles of various causes of red deer deaths were estimated. The major factors were hunting harvest (46% of mortality) and predation (40%, mainly by wolves, but also lynx, and – occasionally – stray dogs). Disease and starvation contributed 9% to deer mortality, and were recorded usually during winter time. Poachers caused 5% of deaths and traffic accident – 1%. Such a strong impact of hunters on deer numbers was a consequence of an elevated harvest in the 1990's, compared with earlier and later years. This was due to foresters' appeals to reduce damage caused by ungulates in forest replantations.

Deer and forest regeneration

In many areas of Europe, red deer browse so heavily on young trees that forests are unable to regenerate. Under these circumstances, red deer often are heavily managed by humans to allow regeneration of trees. However, as previously discussed, most red deer populations in Europe occur in altered habitat with large predators absent. This raises the question, "Do red deer influence the regeneration of forests under natural conditions?"

To help answer this question, the effects of browsing are being investigated in Białowieża National Park (Photo 7.2). First, young trees are being inventoried to determine which tree species are preferred by large herbivores in the forest. Initial results are quite compelling. Mean density of the young tree generation (diameter at breast height, dbh <8 cm) was 12,395 individuals per hectare, including 8,074 trees smaller 30 cm of height, 3,930 trees higher than 30 cm but thinner than 2 cm dbh, and 391 trees of dbh between 2 and 8 cm. Altogether, 14 woody species or genera were found in the regeneration. The main species were: hornbeam (48%), ash (13%), maple (10%), spruce (10%) and lime (4%).

The density of trees whose top-twig showed signs of browsing the previous year was 6,673 individual trees per hectare (54% of all young trees). The intensity of browsing by herbivores depended on the tree species and their height, with about 90% of all trees in the height class 0.6–0.9 m being browsed. The most frequently browsed tree was hornbeam (51% of all browsed trees), and other heavily browsed trees included elm, birch, lime, rowan, and ash.

Three types of damage to stem surfaces were recognized: bark-stripping, tree fraying, and broken trees. About 152 individuals per

Photo 7.2. Forest regeneration is being monitored in the natural oldgrowths of Białowieża National Park. Photo by Sławomir Wąsik.

hectare showed signs of bark-stripping from herbivores. The most common type of bark-stripped tree was lime (32% of all stripped trees). There were about 50 frayed trees per hectare, with spruce being the most commonly frayed tree (34% of all frayed trees). There were also about 35 broken trees per hectare, with willow being the most commonly broken tree (40% of all broken trees). Fresh wounds on stem surfaces were found on about 32 young trees per hectare, with most fresh wounds occurring on black alder (31%), spruce (29%), hornbeam (13%), lime (9%), birch (7%), and ash (5%).

Although this information suggests that ungulates do influence forest regeneration in Białowieża National Park, it is important to determine if herbivore browsing negatively affects tree density and growth. Therefore, sample plots were fenced off from herbivores, and these were compared to unfenced plots, where herbivores could freely browse. After two years, the density of trees in regeneration in the fenced plots was 27% larger and the height of regeneration 45% taller than in unfenced plots.

However, in the natural oldgrowth forests over 98% of saplings usually die at an early age anyway, due to competition for light under the canopies of old trees. So this leaves us with the question, "Do deer browse on the 'doomed surplus' or do they actually shape forest regeneration?" Only more long-term research will answer this important question.

Suggested readings

Clutton-Brock T. H., Guiness F. E. and Albon S. D. 1982. Red deer: behavior and ecology of two sexes. The University of Chicago Press.

Jędrzejewska B., Jędrzejewski W., Bunevich A. N., Miłkowski L. and Krasiński Z. A. 1997. Factors shaping population densities and increase rates of ungulates in Białowieża Primeval Forest (Poland and Belarus) in the 19th and 20th centuries. Acta Theriologica 42: 399–451.

Miścicki S. 1996. Forest regeneration and its damage by herbivorous ungulates in the Białowieża National Park. [In: Biodiversity protection of Białowieża Primeval Forest. P. Paschalis and S. Zajączkowski, eds]. Fundacja "Rozwój SGGW", Warszawa: 91–108.

Okarma H., Jędrzejewska B., Jędrzejewski W., Krasiński Z. A. and Miłkowski L. 1995. The roles of predation, snow cover, acorn crop, and man-related factors on ungulate mortality in Białowieża Primeval Forest, Poland. Acta Theriologica 40: 197–217.

Post E., Langvatn R. and Forchhammer M. C. 1999. Environmental variation shapes sexual dimorphism in red deer. Proceedings of the National Academy of Sciences (USA) 96: 4467–4471.

8

Life after death
– scavenging on ungulate carcasses

Nuria Selva

Although rather disgusting to humans, ungulate carcasses are attractive food to over 30 species of mammals and birds, especially during harsh winters. More prevalent than conventionally thought, scavenging plays a key ecological role in European forests.

Carcass supply in a temperate forest

Nearly all vertebrate predators, from ravens to woodpeckers, and from red foxes to shrews, are scavengers to some extent. Originally, in the temperate forests of Europe, where large herbivores and predators were abundant, scavenging was based on a predictable supply of ungulate carcasses. On one side, large predators constantly "supplied" scavengers with the remains of their kills. On the other, disease, starvation and cold, generously provided scavengers with intact corpses of dead ungulates, mainly in winter.

Under natural conditions in European temperate forests, the diversity of carcasses in the ecosystem used to be very high. Firstly, the variety of species within the ungulate community produced carcasses varying in size, from small roe deer to large bison. Secondly, the origin and placement of the carcass, whether dead or killed by predators, and whether exposed in an open glade or well-hidden in dense forest, determined its state and accessibility to scavengers.

Kills of large predators are among the favourite food of most scavengers. Wolves devour their prey, mainly red deer, usually within one day (see Chapter 10). The amount of remains left for scavengers varies, on average, between 10 and 35% of the ungulate live mass. Remains include entrails (mainly stomach and intestines), skin, large bones (especially the head, legs and backbone) and some flesh. These remnants are relatively easy to find for scavengers because they are usually spread around, the ground is covered in blood and wolf tracks (especially visible in snow) and a strong scent emanates from the kill (Photo 8.1). In the case of big-sized preys, wolves often consume it partially, returning later to finish it. Scavengers take then the opportunity to remove as much as they can during periods when wolves are absent. Most wolf kills are found within hours by scavengers.

Photo 8.1. Types of ungulate carcasses: (A) dead bison; (B) typical view of a wolf kill – the ground covered by blood is especially visible in the snow; (C) roe deer killed by lynx and camouflaged against scavengers; and (D) wild boar shot and discarded by hunters. Photos by Adam Wajrak (A) and Nuria Selva (B, C, D).

Contrary to wolf packs, solitary lynx feed on a kill (mainly roe deer) for several days, and carefully camouflage it to fool scavengers (see Chapter 11). Lynx will drag a carcass to a concealed place, and cover it with grass, litter, leaves, moss, snow and deer hair (Photo 8.1); they reportedly even cache their prey up in trees. In spite of these efforts, some scavengers, mainly wild boar, manage to discover lynx kills and take them over.

In the case of ungulates that die of starvation, disease or cold, scavengers are faced with the difficulty of opening an intact corpse, which often has tough and thick skin. Additionally, there is the risk of disease and parasite transmission. In recent periods, man-caused mortalities (road-casualties and hunting) represent another supply of carrion, which scavengers have quickly learned to exploit (Photo 8.1).

Whereas kills from large predators are supplied to scavengers at a similar rate year round, natural deaths due to malnutrition, sickness or extreme cold temperatures peak at the end of the winter. Between 44 and 71% of these deaths occur from February to March, when many animals have depleted their fat reserves. However, the supply of ungulate carcasses is highly variable from year to year. This supply depends on several factors: density of ungulates, density of large predators, game management, winter severity, and oak seed crops. Extremely severe winters (low temperatures and deep snow cover) can cause mass mortality of ungulates, especially wild boar, which must root for food in the soil. More than 2,400 ungulate carcasses were recorded in Białowieża Forest during the severe

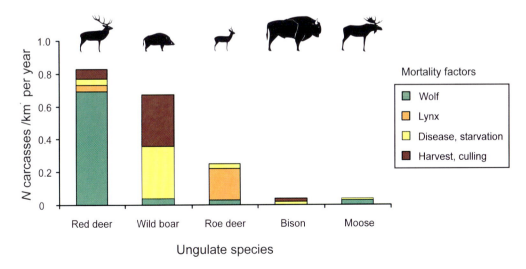

Figure 8.1. Annual supply of ungulate carcasses in Białowieża Forest, expressed as number of carcasses per km^2 per year for each ungulate species, along with main mortality factors.

winter of 1969/70. Wild boar survival is also affected by the acorn crop. A heavy acorn crop leads to an increase in wild boar numbers (due to good reproduction), many of which die the following year when oak trees are barren. From 1998 to 2000, censuses of ungulate carcasses showed that approximately 2 ungulates per km^2 per year were available to scavengers. As expected from their share of the living ungulate community, the most abundant carcasses were of red deer and wild boar, whereas bison and moose were the rarest (Figure 8.1). The most numerous carcasses were red deer killed by wolves, wild boar dead from disease or starvation, wild boar shot and abandoned by hunters, and roe deer killed by lynx.

A diverse guild of scavengers

As many as 33 species of birds and mammals have been documented scavenging on ungulate carcasses in Białowieża Forest. The monitoring of 141 ungulate carcasses from 1997 to 2002 revealed that the main scavengers were: common raven (recorded at 84% of carcasses), red fox (83%), raccoon dog (50%), wolf (47%), jay (45%), wild boar (42%), common buzzard (40%), pine marten (34%), white--tailed eagle (31%), small passerines – mainly tits (24%), and stray dog (13%) (Photo 8.2). Occasional scavengers (visiting less than 10% of ungulate carcasses) were shrews, rodents, badger, magpie, goshawk, lynx, polecat, golden eagle, weasel, red squirrel, stoat, lesser--spotted eagle, great spotted woodpecker, crow, and sparrowhawk. Among small passerines, the great and blue tit were commonly recorded feeding from carcasses in winter, while other birds, such as the chaffinch and blackbird, were exclusively observed in summer when feeding on maggots in rotten carrion. Other avian scavengers recorded in Białowieża Forest were the crested tit, yellowhammer, tawny owl, and hobby. Ravens, wolves, raccoon dogs, jays, wild boar and great tits usually fed at carcasses in groups. All species preferentially utilized ungulate carcasses during the cold season, with the exception of wolves and raccoon dogs. Wolves scavenged more frequently from the end of winter till mid summer.

The scavenging guild of temperate forests is not completely opportunistic. Scavenger preferences are influenced by carcass origin and placement, and the species of ungulate. Ravens and red foxes are adapted to find wolf kills. Pine martens, which can fall prey to lynx, are also more fond of wolf than lynx kills. The wild boar shows a strong preference for predator kills, avoiding animals dead from natural causes (Photo 8.2). Raccoon dogs show some preference for ungulates not killed by predators. A good strategy for animals less efficient in locating carcasses is to follow those who are good trackers. In this sense, noisy crowds of ravens are an unmistakable sign for many raptors, especially white-tailed eagles and buzzards.

Weather conditions, mainly ambient temperature and snow cover, affect scavenging frequency. Under conditions of extreme low temperatures and deep snow cover, some species decrease their activity and movements, and do not visit carcasses, while others

Photo 8.2. White-tailed eagle feeding on a wild boar carcass in winter (A). Pine marten scavenging on a wolf kill (B). Wild boar attending a red deer killed by wolves (C). Photos by Adam Wajrak (A, C) and Thomas Müller (B).

abruptly increase scavenging. The habitat in which the carcass is located also influences the presence of scavengers. Raptors, mainly buzzards and white-tailed eagles, are more common at carcasses located in open glades. Pine martens and raccoon dogs are frequently observed at carcasses under the forest canopy.

The time of depletion of a carcass is highly variable. It ranges from one day, in the case of a young ungulate killed by wolves, to more than 3 months for dead bison (Figure 8.2). Several factors contribute to these differences: the carcass' initial weight; the cause of death (predator kill versus other), and the season. On average, scavengers consume 2.5 kg daily, but the maximum amount scavenged in one day was 68 kg from a bison carcass.

No doubt, the largest and most conspicuous carcasses in Białowieża Forest are those of bison. They provide scavengers with more than 400 kg of meat for at least 100 days. However, none of the medium- and small-sized scavengers can feed on a bison carcass unless wolves create an opening in its thick, tough skin. Bison carcasses are extremely attractive for wolves, which visit them repeatedly. During these visits, wolves progressively make more parts accessible to other scavengers, and trigger their scavenging activity. Especially foxes and raccoon dogs, attend bison carcasses more frequently just after wolves have visited them. Often, scavengers create a "tunnel" in order to consume the carcass from the inside. Consumption of bison carcasses by scavengers is highest in the beginning of carcass exploitation. On average, almost 7 kg are consumed daily during the first two weeks, decreasing to 4 kg during the next two weeks, and progressively declining with time (Figure 8.2). In the last stages of the depletion process, the dismemberment of a

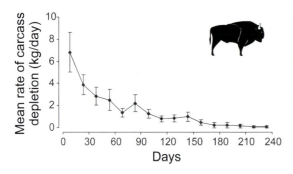

Figure 8.2. Consumption of bison carcasses by scavengers to complete depletion in Białowieża Forest. The graph shows the mean (± SE) daily consumption (kg/day) of bison carcasses per 15-day period. (Reprinted from: *Ecoscience* 10: 303–311, 2003.) Photo by Nuria Selva.

bison carcass begins, partly as a consequence of repeated dragging by wolves. Often, the end of a bison's "second life" comes with the arrival of spring, when microbial and invertebrate activity wipe clean the last remains.

Main scavengers

The ultimate scavenger of temperate forests is the raven. Although its diet consists of anything edible it can catch or pick up, in winter the raven is a specialized scavenger. Ravens closely associate with wolves, which allow them to discover wolf kills almost immediately. Immature ravens aggregate in large flocks and roost communally, but do not forage in groups. They search for food separately and later share information about discovered carcasses. Ravens can actively recruit conspecifics by emitting special types of calls at the carrion site. In addition, ravens remove flesh from carcasses to cache for later use. They often share carcasses with other species, such as foxes, wild boar, buzzards, and white-tailed eagles. However, ravens also mob their commensals, especially raptors, which are often forced to leave the carcasses. Harassment by ravens may include continuously picking at the tail of other scavenging birds. Only does the goshawk seem to dominate over raven flocks at the carrion.

Half the monitored carcasses were discovered by ravens on the first day, and 75% were discovered on the second day. However, there was a manifest habitat segregation between flocks of immatures and territorial pairs when exploiting large-sized carcasses. Bison carcasses located under the forest canopy were utilized exclusively by territorial pairs, whereas those located in open glades were accessible also to flocks (Photo 8.1). Only in the cases of well-concealed carcasses, such as lynx kills, may ravens fail to find them. Ravens have learned to follow hunters in order to immediately gorge themselves on deer and boar entrails discarded by hunters in the forest.

In early autumn, ravens increase their scavenging activity and keep it very high during the whole winter, finally shifting to other food in spring (Figure 8.3). The mean number of ravens observed at a carcass followed the same seasonal pattern. In the warm season (during the breeding period), carcasses were usually attended by raven pairs. During the rest of the year, the mean number of ravens seen at a carcass increased between 5 and 10 (the maximum observed in Białowieża Forest was 60 ravens). Ravens are so dependent on ungulate carcasses in the cold period, that in many European forests without ungulate carrion, raven calls are no longer heard.

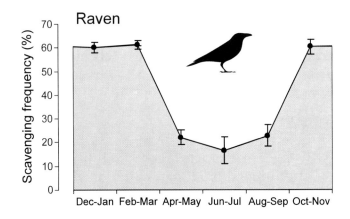
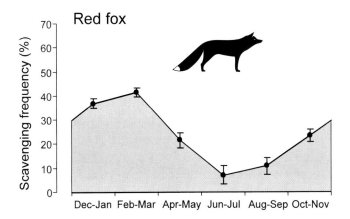
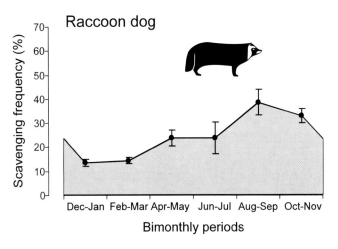

Figure 8.3. Variation in the scavenging frequency (%) of main scavengers throughout the year (shaded area). Each point denotes the percentage (± SE) of monitoring inspections at carcasses, with a given scavenger recorded.

The red fox is the most important mammalian scavenger of temperate forests. Foxes also follow wolves in order to find the remains of their kills. But this is a risky habit, therefore when feeding on large predator kills, foxes must be alert and cautious. They also spend as little time as possible at carcasses. In Białowieża Forest, foxes were observed to leave a carcass with pieces of meat so big, sometimes they could hardly carry them away. Foxes rarely scavenge on lynx kills as the lynx usually stay near and guard it. Foxes also actively search for dead wild boar by visiting their lairs. They are highly efficient at discovering carcasses; on average, it took them 2.5 days to find half the monitored carcasses. Foxes utilized carcasses located in the forest and in open areas with the same intensity. Like ravens, foxes are quite fond of caching food, and when possible, raiding caches made by others, including those of ravens. In Białowieża Forest, they were documented retrieving previously cached food once every 10 km of trail.

Though the predominant item in fox diets are voles (40% of biomass consumed), ungulate carcasses are the second most important food resource, making up 26% of biomass consumed throughout the year. Their scavenging is most frequent in late winter, when rodents are scarce and difficult to capture due to thick snow cover. Foxes usually forage alone and they often urinate or defecate at depleted ungulate carcasses.

The raccoon dog is the only exotic scavenger in the guild (Photo 8.3). It appeared in Białowieża Forest in the 1950's, from the European part of the former Soviet Union, where it was introduced as a

Photo 8.3. The raccoon dog, one of the main mammalian scavengers. Photo by Rafał Kowalczyk.

valuable furbearer. More than predators, they are often defined as "gatherers" and opportunistic omnivores. Ungulate carcasses play a prime role in raccoon dog diets in Białowieża Forest. They do not show any preferences for carcass types, which are consumed as they become available. Slow and clumsy animals, raccoon dogs are in danger of being killed when scavenging. They are victims of host predators, such as wolves and lynx, and other scavengers, such as white-tailed eagles and stray dogs. Raccoon dogs usually visit carcasses in pairs or family groups.

One of the most characteristic features of raccoon dog's life habits is their inactivity during winter. However, during spells of mild weather, they wake up and actively search for ungulate carcasses. In autumn and winter, ungulate carrion amounts to 56% of the biomass consumed by raccoon dogs. Because of their low activity in winter, raccoon dogs were recorded at carcasses more often during the warm period, especially in late summer and early autumn (Figure 8.3). In the warm season, carrion makes up 29% of their food biomass.

Although our knowledge about the role of carrion resources in ecosystems is still very limited, undoubtedly scavenging processes were an important part of the food web dynamics in temperate forests. Nowadays, we can observe them in only a few places, such as Białowieża Primeval Forest, where a great diversity of ungulates and other vertebrates coexist.

Suggested readings

DeVault T. L., Rhodes O. E. and Shivik J. A. 2003. Scavenging by vertebrates: behavioral, ecological and evolutionary perspectives on an important energy transfer pathway in terrestrial ecosystems. Oikos 102: 225–234.

Heinrich B. 1990. Ravens in winter. Barrie and Jenkins, London.

Jędrzejewska B. and Jędrzejewski W. 1998. Scavenging – seemingly a "free lunch" sometimes at high cost. [In: Predation in vertebrate communities. The Białowieża Primeval Forest as a case study.] Springer Verlag, Berlin: 411–420.

Jędrzejewski W. and Jędrzejewska B. 1998. Foraging and diet of the red fox *Vulpes vulpes* in relation to variable food resources in Białowieża National Park, Poland. Ecography 16: 47–64.

Selva N., Jędrzejewska B., Jędrzejewski W. and Wajrak A. 2003. Scavenging on European bison carcasses in Białowieża Primeval Forest (eastern Poland). Ecoscience 10: 303–311.

9

The brown bear
– a story without a happy ending

Tomasz Samojlik

A monstrous brown bear jumped on the bison's back, clutched the bull's neck with its strong paws, and nearly rode it in a deadly duel. Villagers from Białowieża Forest would swear that during this struggle, the two giants destroyed all trees and bushes in a 200-m radius. It was the year 1844. The worst time for such a story to occur, and a turning point in the history of brown bears in Białowieża Forest.

Animalia superiora – the beast for royal hunts

Vast forests are the main habitats of brown bears, where they occupy home ranges covering 20 to 500 km². Thus, Białowieża Primeval Forest was an ideal home for them. However, the history of bears in Białowieża Forest, to put it shortly, fluctuated from the strict protection of bears as valuable game for monarchal hunts (until the 18th century), to deliberate extermination of these animals in the 19th century, and finally to an attempt at restituting their numbers (undertaken in 1937). By the 20th century, however, Białowieża Forest suffered such significant destruction and political divisions, that it was no longer suitable habitat for bears.

In mediaeval times, when forests and swamps covered large areas of Poland, big game hunting was legally reserved only for the monarchs and nobility. During so-called *venatio magna*, great hunts, the land's most valuable game animals were chased. This group of *animalia superiora* included aurochs, European bison, moose, red deer, and brown bears. Kings and dukes from the Piast and Jagiellonian dynasties devoted significant amounts of time to hunting, which – in addition to serving the important role of delivering food to the monarch's court and army – was exciting entertainment and sport. Białowieża Forest, which from the 14th–18th century had the status as a royal hunting ground, was one of the favourite hunting places for kings and dukes of the Polish-Lithuanian Commonwealth.

The first bear hunt in Białowieża Forest was described by Jan Długosz, the 15th century Polish historian in his *"Annales seu cronicae incliti regni Poloniae"*. In 1426, king Władysław Jagiełło, with his entire court, came to Białowieża seeking shelter from the black death plague threatening Cracow, the Polish capital at that time: *"Anno Domini 1426. King of Poland Władysław, having spent Christmas day in Wilno with his wife Queen Zofia, as the plague has gone, was going to travel back to the Polish Kingdom from Lithuania before the end of carnival. While chasing a bear in the hunting place named Białowieże, the King broke his leg by accident"*.

Dangerous beasts as they were, brown bears repeatedly appeared as the culprits in old chronicles and reports. In 1581, an unfortunate accident happened during king Stefan Batory's bear hunt. A bear, scared away from its lair, attacked and wounded a boy

Figure 9.1. Bear caught in a net in Poland. (Reprint of a drawing by an unknown author, 18th century; from the collection of the Princes Czartoryski Foundation at the National Museum of Cracow.)

who took part in the battue. King Batory paid generous compensation for the unlucky boy.

Since the 16th century, in the woodlands of the Great Lithuanian Duchy, bears were captured alive in nets, like the one shown in Figure 9.1, and then transported to royal or magnate castles for arena fights composed of various beasts. On 19 September 1637, a spectacular bear fight was organised at the Royal Castle in Warsaw, adding splendour to the wedding of king Władysław IV Waza. Giovanni Battista Tartaglini, a royal guest, witnessed the event: *"In one of the Royal Castle's courtyards (...) bears wrestled various animals. Usually five bears were let out and fought two horses (...), a bull, old bison (...). Also bears struggled with each other, but without much effort and damage. In the end all five, one after another, were attacked by three dogs, aided by an additional two in case of a wilder bear, and after having fought awhile, the bears were killed with one strong spear blow by the Hunting Master"*.

In 1705, a hunt organized for king August II Wettin took place in Białowieża Forest. The king, famous for his unusual physical vigour, was armed only with a spear when he chased after a brown bear. The bear suddenly stopped and attacked, throwing his majesty down. It took all the king's legendary strength to escape from the bear's clutch.

The brown bear as a pest

In the 18th century, brown bears in Białowieża Forest were also targeted by gentry and game wardens because of their valuable pelts, and not least of all due to their occasional raids on cattle and bee-hives. The brown bear is an omnivorous species, adapted to both a herbivorous and carnivorous diet. In the spring, they frequently scavenge on carrion or hunt for other animals, occasionally as big as deer and cattle. Later, in summer and autumn the share of vegetable matter in their diet increases. Being omnivorous, bears are often attracted to farms, pastures and gardens, where they turn into a pest, predating on livestock and raiding plantations. In Białowieża Forest, the main complaint against bears was that they affected the traditional and much-valued forest bee-keeping.

In the late 18th century, numerous apiaries with nearly 1,000 bee-hives existed in Białowieża Forest, either in the form of cavities hollowed in old trees, or in the form of log fragments placed in trees, sometimes on special platforms. Their owners tried to protect the bees with special constructions. In the case of bee-hives in cavities, an oak log was hung on a tree trunk in front of the bee-hive, covering it. When a bear pushed aside the log and tried reaching for honey, the log worked as a pendulum and swung back, hitting the bear. Moreover, trees with bee-hives could be surrounded with sharpened stakes. Yet another way to deter bears was to build a platform around a trunk beneath a bee-hive. But even the most elaborate protection systems sometimes failed. In September 1780, artist Jan Henryk Müntz was visiting Białowieża Forest and witnessed a brown bear that damaged an arboreal apiary. Müntz, not only depicted the situation (Figure 9.2), but also described it: "*What you can see here is the bear that has climbed an oak, where 24 very well protected bee-hives stood. However, once it had eaten and destroyed all of the apiary, the bear was not able to get down. It was shot by the bee-hives' owners. It was a specimen of the biggest, brown kind. It was first kept alive for a few days, guarded by peasants like a true criminal. On the last day, I saw it alive in the tree, making funny faces to all the gathered people, who covered a distance of a few miles to see the honey thief and to gladden themselves about the capture*".

Bear hunts continued after the third partition of Poland in 1795, when Białowieża Forest fell under Russian rule. In 1821 and 1823, Julius von Brincken, the main forest manager of the Polish Kingdom under Russian rule, came for several hunts to Białowieża Forest. He was interested in virtually all game animals, and shot

Figure 9.2. "The bear hunt" in Białowieża Forest in September 1780. (Reprint of a watercolour by J. H. Müntz, 1783, from the collection of the Print Room of the Warsaw University Library.)

bison and moose. However, his attempts to kill a brown bear failed. Instead, he was given the chance to taste bear ham during a breakfast at the local forester's house in February 1823: *"On 13 February we went to the [Białowieża] Forest to reach the King's Bridge [Królowy Most], where lived a forester, and where the hunters gathered. On the next day, we ate breakfast as admirable as the surrounding forest. It was made up of bear ham, moose meat, wild boar, and a young European bison, mutilated by wolves the previous day".*

The tradition of serving bear ham and paws survived in Polish kitchens until the early 20th century. *"The Great Illustrated Encyclopaedia"* printed in 1903, brings the following description of a meal: *"Today, even if bear paws are served at the table, they come only in cold jelly, cooked similarly to pork legs. The difference is that bear paws are served whole, so that guests can see that the dish contains no other thing except the bear paws. Their appearance reminds that of a human foot, which makes some people unable to even taste this particular delicacy".*

Management to the point of extinction

Walerian Kurowski, author of the hunting guide ("Hunting in Poland and Lithuania", Poznań, 1865), describes the methods of hunting

Figure 9.3. Bear attacking a bison in the Białowieża Forest. (Drawing by N. Samokish, reprinted from: *Belovezhskaja Pushcha*. St. Petersburg, 1903.)

bears used in Białowieża Forest from 1820–1830. "*A pit 7 by 7 ells [approx. 4 m] and 7 ells deep should be dug (...), the walls of the pit must be lined with boards 4 inches thick and perfectly shaved, so the bear will not be able to climb up with its claws (...). Over the pit two thick poles are put (...) and on their crossing a pot with honey is placed. From above the pit is covered with thin branches.*" This method was reported to Kurowski by Eugeniusz de Ronke, the chief forester of Białowieża Forest, who assured the author of its effectiveness, as bears were capable of smelling the honey from a long distance.

It was only in the mid 19th century that brown bears became the target of deliberate extermination. At that time, Białowieża Forest under the Russian rule witnessed the introduction of a game management system which promoted ungulates (especially the European bison) and heavily controlled all predators. The brown bear, the largest and rarest carnivore, being an effective predator of bison, became the first victim of the new management rules. Game reports, published by Georgii Karcov, in 1903, documented that during the period 1832–1873, bears killed 12 bison (Figure 9.3). Karcov described the massive extermination programme of large predators that started in 1869. Until 1878, in a total of 166 round-up hunts, five bears were killed. No more bears were seen in the forest, despite the fact that until the 1890 an extra bounty of 50 rubels was offered to anyone who shot a bear.

Tame bears do not like the forest

The decision to reintroduce brown bears in Białowieża Forest took a long time to mature. In the meantime, the political situation changed. Poland, after over 120 years, regained independence in 1918. Białowieża Forest was administered by the Polish General Directorate of State Forests, which in 1937 decided to reintroduce bears. It was a two-part plan: some bears were to be brought to Białowieża Forest, and at the same time a captive breeding programme was established here. The programme was led by the director of Białowieża National Park, Jan J. Karpiński.

Lola, a pregnant female, was transported to Białowieża National Park from the Poznań zoo, and put in a large cage. After a pregnancy of 6–8 months, female bears give birth during hibernation between December and February. Lola whelped two cubs in January 1938. At the same time, 4 cubs were bought in the Soviet Union and set free in the forest. Unfortunately, they were tame, not afraid of humans, and hardly able to find food on their own (Photo 9.1). Their friendly behaviour encouraged foresters and visitors to feed and pet them, but eventually it led to fatal consequences. In search of food they often approached people, demolished houses, and would rob food from a moose enclosure. As similar events continued, one cub was killed by villagers, and another was sent to the Warsaw zoo. Four new bears were brought to Białowieża Forest, but these were tame animals as well, and they met the same fate as the previous group. Worse still, in 1938, one of the bears attacked a girl collecting berries. Luckily, she was saved by a tourist who heard her screams. Probably, only one or two of the tame bears learnt to live in the wild and survived longer.

Lola's two cubs (a male and a female) born in the wild, had better chances of adapting to Białowieża Forest. In nature, mortality of cubs in the first year reaches about 50%. Fortunately, Lola's offspring survived. The bars of their cage were bent in a way that enabled them to go out and in, but kept the mother inside. The cubs were gradually separated from her, and became independent. Soon, Lola was taken to another part of the forest.

When World War II broke out, the reintroduction of bears was at risk. The Soviets, occupying the area from 1939–1941, were not interested in bears, but tolerated rangers from Białowieża feeding Lola. In 1941, Lola was freed from her cage. Later, she was seen in the forest with a male bear. In June 1941, Germans took over Białowieża Forest and transformed it into the Third Reich's Hunting

Photo 9.1. Bears reintroduced into Białowieża Forest from 1938–1939. Photo by Jan J. Karpiński, from the collection of the Białowieża National Park.

Reserve. Five more bears of unknown origin were brought here. The action, badly organized and not co-ordinated, soon led to tragedy: in 1942, a bear killed two people in the forest. Soon after, almost all bears fell victim to poachers.

In 1945, a new Polish-Soviet border divided the Białowieża Forest. Tracks from a single bear were repeatedly observed on the Soviet (Belarussian) side until 1950. As bears in the wild may live up to 30 years, it is probable that they were the tracks of one of Lola's cubs. The last bear tracks were seen in Białowieża Forest in 1963, when a bear – probably dispersing from a population in north-eastern Belarus – crossed the Polish-Soviet border. After that event, nothing was heard from brown bears in Białowieża Forest.

During the whole reintroduction period, at least two litters were born in the wild. Bears survived here for 13 years (1938–1950). This indicates that the restitution process could have been successful, if only the circumstances were more favourable and the times more peaceful. Nowadays, listed in the Polish Red Data Book of Animals, bears occur in Poland only in the Carpathian Mountains, where their population is estimated at 100–130 individuals.

Human mistakes in dealing with nature can be corrected. For example, though it took a lot of time and effort, the restitution of bison was crowned a success. However, some damage seems hardly repairable, as brown bears no longer roam the woodlands of Białowieża Forest. The question is, will they get another chance in the future?

Suggested readings

Brincken J. 1826. Memoire descriptif sur la foret imperiale de Białowieża, en Lithuanie. N. Glucksberg, Varsovie. [In French]

Jakubiec Z. and Buchalczyk T. 1987. The brown bear in Poland: its history and present numbers. Acta Theriologica 32: 289–306.

Karcov G. 1903. Belovezshkaya Pushcha, ee istoricheskii ocherk, sovremennoe okhotniche khozistvo i Vysochaishiya okhoty v Pushche [Belovezha Primeval Forest. Historical description, contemporary game management, and monarchial hunts in the Forest]. F. A. Marks, Sankt-Petersburg. [In Russian]

Karpiński J. J. 1949. O niedźwiedziach w Puszczy Białowieskiej [On the bears in Białowieża Primeval Forest]. Chrońmy Przyrodę Ojczystą 4–6: 35–41. [In Polish]

Kryštufek B., Flajšman B. and Griffiths H. I. 2003. Living with bears. A large European carnivore in a shrinking world. Ecological Forum of the Liberal Democracy of Slovenia, Lubljana.

10

Wolves' predation on deer

Włodzimierz Jędrzejewski and Bogumiła Jędrzejewska

In most of their vast Holarctic range, wolves prey primarily on ungulates. It is rare, however, for these carnivores to co-exist with more than 2–3 species of potential prey. Białowieża Primeval Forest harbours five ungulate species, ranging in size from 20 to over 500 kilograms. Wolves can successfully hunt all these species, but they tend to specialise on just one, the red deer. Such selective predation by wolves has profound consequences for deer population dynamics.

Wolf hunting territories

Wolves live in packs, family units usually comprising an adult breeding pair and their juvenile and subadult offspring. In Białowieża Forest, the typical packs contain 4–5 wolves, although packs of 2 to 10 wolves have been recorded. Each pack maintains an exclusive territory. A radio-telemetry study conducted in the Polish section of Białowieża Forest revealed that the annual territories of wolf packs covered from 140 to 320 km^2, on average 220 km^2 (Figure 10.1). The most important area is the breeding den, and a core zone surrounding the den. Pups are born in late April and early May. They stay in their natal den for about 3 weeks, and until late June the females with pups utilise 1–2 other dens or shelters located within 1–2 kilometres of the breeding den. During that time, the lives of all pack members are concentrated around the dens, as the pups require virtually constant care and attendance by the female or another pack member. The areas used by wolves for hunting on consecutive days overlapped extensively. The territory of a pack may

Photo 10.1. Male wolf in winter in Białowieża Forest. Photo by Włodzimierz Jędrzejewski.

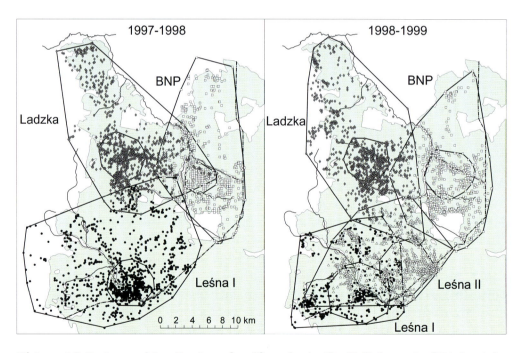

Figure 10.1. Annual territories of wolf packs in the Polish part of Białowieża Forest. Points are radio-tracking locations (1 May – 30 April), and polygons are Minimum Convex Polygons embracing 100% and 50% of locations. In the winter season 1997/1998, the Leśna I pack split into two packs. Green area denotes forests.

shrink to a mere 20–30 km² in May–June. From late summer, when the young begin to travel with other pack members, the range used by wolves increases to reach the maximum size in winter. In the cold season, wolves (Photo 10.1) move widely and utilise their territory in a rotational manner (Figure 10.2), returning to the same areas every 6 days on average. Rotational use is related to intense patrolling and territory defence, especially prior to and during the mating season in January–February, but may also help wolves to avoid behavioural disturbance of prey.

While the seasonal variation in territory size is governed by the breeding cycle of wolves (mating, birth and rearing of pups), the among-pack and between-year variation in wolf territory size is generally shaped by the abundance of ungulates, the wolves' main prey. With lower densities of ungulates, wolves have to travel longer distances to make a kill, covering larger areas. Radio-tracking showed

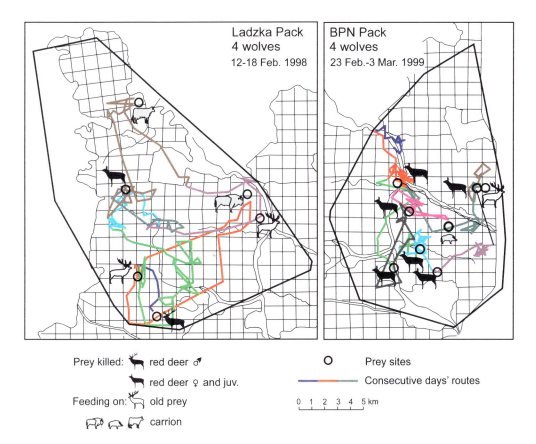

Figure 10.2. Wolf territories, examples of daily routes and sequences of prey killed and scavenged upon during 6–9 days by two wolf packs studied by radio-tracking in Białowieża Forest.

that, on average, the daily route of a wolf pack was 23 km (range 0.5–64 km). In 1994–2000, three to four packs were recorded in the Polish part of Białowieża Forest (Figure 10.1) and wolf population density was 2–3 individuals per 100 km^2.

Predation impact

In 1985–1999, the proportion of the biomass consumed by wolves in Białowieża Forest consisting of ungulates did not drop below 90% and in some years it reached 99%. Wolves could successfully hunt ungulates of all species, from the smallest roe deer and piglets of wild boar to adult female bison. However, their most strongly preferred prey was the red deer, constituting 70% of all ungulates killed (Photo 10.2). Sporadically, wolves also killed medium- and small-sized animals such as beavers, raccoon dogs, brown hares, red foxes, rodents, or frogs. In addition, they occasionally scavenged on the discarded carcasses of domestic animals (cattle and pigs), and the carcasses of wild boar and European bison.

To estimate their kill rates, we tracked the locations of radio--collared wolves continuously day and night (for a total of 323 days) and later we searched the areas where wolves had remained sedentary for potential prey remains. The mean kill rate of a typical pack consisting of 4–5 wolves was one prey per 2 days, as estimated from

Photo 10.2. Red deer stag killed by wolves in Białowieża Forest. Photo by Włodzimierz Jędrzejewski.

the time intervals between consecutive kills we found in the forest. The larger the killed prey, the more time elapsed before the wolves attempted their next kill (Figure 10.3). In terms of prey species, a pack of wolves killed one red deer every 3 days, plus one wild boar every 7 days, and one other (usually smaller) animal once a month. Wolves typically covered 40–50 km from one successful hunt to the next (see Figure 10.2). Most hunts occurred at night, usually before sunrise or after sunset.

The kill rate did not depend on the number of wolves in a hunting group (a range of 2–6 wolves), but larger packs tended to hunt for larger prey more often than the small packs. In consequence, the amount of food acquired per wolf was very similar in small and large packs. Daily food intake varied from 4 to 9 kg of meat per wolf, or on average 5.6 kg. The kill rate of wolves increased markedly with snow cover. Deep snow impeded deer movement and as the deer, especially calves, weakened, they became more susceptible to predation.

What is the role of wolf predation in red deer population of Białowieża Forest? Based on the kill rates and densities of wolves, we estimated that they annually took a mean of 72 deer from 100 km^2, which constituted 12% of spring (seasonally highest) densities of deer.

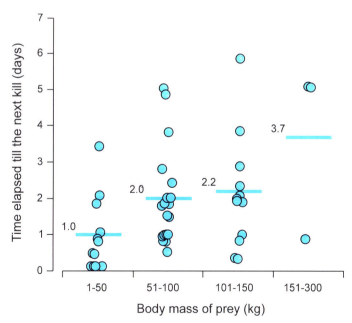

Figure 10.3. Time elapsed before the next kill in relation to the body mass of prey. Circles show time intervals between consecutive kills by wolves. Horizontal bars and numbers indicate mean values. (Reprinted from: *Ecology* 83: 1341–1356, 2002; modified.)

Wolf predation was equivalent to 40% of deer annual increase due to breeding and 40% of their annual mortality figures. By eliminating a fair proportion of deer production every year, wolves hampered the population growth of red deer and prolonged the time of their reaching the habitat's carrying capacity. Furthermore, predation by lynx and the hunting harvest by humans were also important factors limiting deer numbers in Białowieża Forest (see Chapter 7).

Wolves, deer, and humans

Between 1994–1999, when the radio-telemetry study was conducted, wolves were protected in the Polish section of Białowieża Forest. Though poaching did occur, wolf populations were fairly stable, or even slightly increasing in numbers. However, this situation was not typical for the long-term dynamics of wolf populations. The last 150 years exemplify the entangled history of wolves and man. During the times of war and chaos, wolves flourished and their densities reached up to 7–9 individuals per 100 km^2 (Figure 10.4). Peace and prosperity in human society usually corresponded to times of peril for wolves. In Białowieża Forest, the most severe wolf control was followed by their temporal extermination from the area in 1880–1915

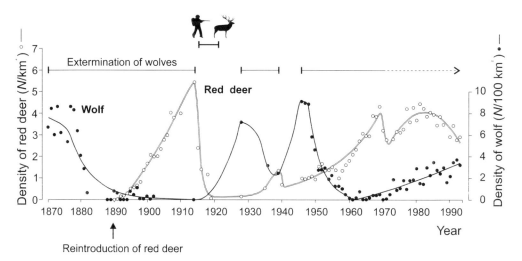

Figure 10.4. Population dynamics of red deer and wolves in the whole Białowieża Forest between 1870–1993. Periods of wolf extermination are marked by thin lines, and years of heavy though not exterminating control by a thin broken line. Years of heavy exploitation of red deer by poachers and soldiers during World War I are marked by a thick line. Points are empirical data and lines are smoothed population dynamics. (Reprinted from: *Predation in vertebrate communities*, 1998, Springer Verlag; modified.)

and 1946–1970. Since the 1970's, wolves have recolonised Białowieża Forest from the east. In the Polish section of Białowieża Forest, wolves have been protected since 1989. In the Belarussian part, wolves have still been treated as pests and every winter a high proportion of wolves is shot during traditional hunts with 'fladry' (a line of flags on ropes).

On a long time scale, the population of red deer has also undergone dramatic fluctuations. Extinct previous to 1800, probably due to a cooling of the regional climate, the species was absent from Białowieża Forest for nearly a century. In 1890, it was reintroduced, but uncontrolled exploitation between 1915–1921, in the years of war, revolution and political unrest, had again threatened its survival (Figure 10.4).

Interestingly, when population dynamics of wolves is transposed on that of red deer, it appears that growth and decline in deer numbers alternates with wolf density. Extermination of wolves during 1880–1915 had cleared the ground for the reintroduction of red deer and allowed for an exponential increase in deer numbers. Between 1915–1921, deer were nearly extirpated by humans. Wolves – relieved from predator control during the First and the Second World Wars – grew in numbers and limited the deer population to a very low density for over 30 years. Red deer numbers increased only after the second wave of wolf extermination that began in the late 1940's (Figure 10.4). In summary, the long-term data set from Białowieża Forest shows that when not controlled by humans, wolves effectively limit red deer density below the capacity set by food resources.

Contrary to typical predator-prey relationships, wolf densities did not depend strongly on red deer availability. Wolf numbers did not decline when deer became scarce, as they were able to exploit the buffer prey species of wild boar, roe deer, and livestock, and in the 19th century European bison. Indeed, selective hunting on red deer combined with generalist feeding habits have made wolves a serious threat to deer in Europe's temperate woodlands. This very feature of wolf ecology often leads to conflicts with hunters, who see the wolves as executioners of red deer and competitors for their trophies.

Suggested readings

Jędrzejewska B., Jędrzejewski W., Bunevich A. N., Miłkowski L. and Okarma H. 1996. Population dynamics of wolves *Canis lupus* in Białowieża Primeval Forest (Poland and Belarus) in relation to hunting by humans, 1847–1993. Mammal Review 26: 103–126.

Jędrzejewska B. and Jędrzejewski W. 1998. Predation in vertebrate communities. The Białowieża Primeval Forest as a case study. Springer Verlag, Berlin: 1–450.

Jędrzejewski W., Jędrzejewska B., Okarma H., Schmidt K., Zub K. and Musiani M. 2000. Prey selection and predation by wolves in Białowieża Primeval Forest, Poland. Journal of Mammalogy 81: 197–212.

Jędrzejewski W., Schmidt K., Theuerkauf J., Jędrzejewska B. and Okarma H. 2001. Daily movements and territory use by radio-collared wolves (*Canis lupus*) in Białowieża Primeval Forest in Poland. Canadian Journal of Zoology 79: 1993–2004.

Jędrzejewski W., Schmidt K., Theuerkauf J., Jędrzejewska B., Selva N., Zub K. and Szymura L. 2002. Kill rates and predation by wolves on ungulatepopulations in Białowieża Primeval Forest (Poland). Ecology 83: 1341–1356.

11

The large cat in Europe

Krzysztof Schmidt

The lynx – a large, wild and powerful carnivorous mammal, has the strength to kill an adult female deer. In search of its prey, this lone hunter undertakes long routes over vast areas of contiguous forests. But is it equally strong to survive in a modern European landscape? Are there still enough space and prey resources for this rare cat?

Searching for prey

At dusk a lynx leaves its shelter in the dense bush and slowly walks the forest trail (Photo 11.1). It heads towards the site of its last successful hunt, where prey remains have been concealed under a fallen tree. The lynx is exclusively carnivorous. It hunts for prey as small as rodents, hares and birds, but also as large as red deer. However, its most preferred prey are small- or medium-sized ungulates. In the Palaearctic zone, these are the roe deer, chamois, musk deer and sika deer – species of similar size or slightly larger than the lynx itself. They are not too large for the 20-kg cat to tackle, yet large enough to provide food for a long period.

In Białowieża Forest, roe deer are the main prey of lynx, with calf and female red deer providing buffer prey. A single kill provides a lynx with meals for a few days. On average, each lynx kills 67 ungulates per year, but the number of deer needed to support each lynx differs, depending on sex and age of the cat. The least efficient hunters are subadult individuals, which kill a deer every 8 days and have to supplement their diet with smaller prey. An adult male lynx usually kills ungulates every 5 days. It is, however, an adult female

Photo 11.1. A lynx in Białowieża Forest. Photo by Jan Walencik.

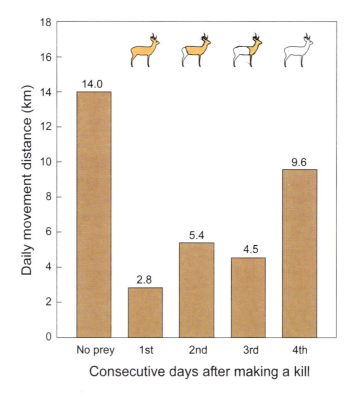

Figure 11.1. Mean daily movement distances of a lynx on a day without a kill, and consecutive days after a kill. The roe deer silhouettes symbolise the amount of prey left uneaten. (Reprinted from: *Annales Zoologici Fennici* 39: 29–41, 2002.)

leading kittens that is the most successful predator. They kill a roe or red deer every second day. A family, consisting of a female with three kittens, consumes almost 200 ungulates each year. This shows that lynx are potentially capable of killing more prey than necessary for one individual, but they only do so when more food is needed for offspring.

As large prey must be consumed over the course of a few days, lynx evolved behaviour to lower the risk of their meals being robbed by other predators or scavengers (see Chapter 8). They often pull the carcass out of sight to hide it among dense bushes or under fallen trees, sometimes several dozen metres from the kill site. Moreover, they cover it with leaves, grass, snow and hairs plucked from the prey. This habit of concealing their prey allows them to leave a kill unattended.

When hunting, lynx do not engage in long pursuits or chases. Instead, after a lynx locates its prey, it leaps just a few times, knocking the victim over with the impetus of its body, and kills with a bite to the throat. If unsuccessful, it quickly abandons the chase. Searching for prey consumes time and energy. Although lynx are regarded as stalk-and-ambush hunters, the real ambush is the last phase of a long hunt, the success of which greatly depends on the density of prey. In Białowieża Forest, even during periods of high roe deer abundance, lynx searching for prey covered, on average, more than 20 kilometres between consecutive kills and most often it took them 2–3 days.

Thus, a successful hunt is a fine reward for this predator, and the first day after making a kill is often a time of leisure. The lynx stays near the kill and may not move at all. However, once the kill is secured and safely hidden, the lynx can begin to search for more prey. This seems to show that the instinct to kill in lynx is ever present. They are increasingly more mobile as they consume their prey, and make bigger efforts to hunt (walk longer distances) when they have no kill in storage (Figure 11.1). Although a lynx may succeed in having more than one kill at a time, they usually do not abandon any of them. In most cases, lynx eat nearly all edible parts of a deer, leaving only large bones and skin.

Solitary roaming over large home ranges

Although lynx – like most felids – are considered solitary, only males fully conform to this perception. They move and hunt alone while avoiding contact with other males. Adult females are usually accompanied by kittens from May till March, and only during the remaining 1–2 months do they move solitarily.

Resident adult males occupy separate home ranges, though they may partly (by 30%) overlap each other (Figure 11.2). However, even in the areas of overlap, encounters between males happen very rarely. Males live separate lives also in relation to females. Though they mostly occupy common areas (the range of a male encompasses one or two female home ranges), they rarely come into contact, except during the mating season in February and March. And then, a male and a female stay together for only 3–5 days.

Female lynx are strongly territorial. Home ranges of neighbouring adult females overlap by just 6%. As they have to provide food for their kittens, these exclusive home ranges may result from stronger competition for food among females.

Lynx home ranges can reach enormous sizes, though they vary greatly due to several factors. Adult males in Białowieża Forest roamed over ranges from 190 to 340 km^2, whereas females used areas almost twice as small (120–150 km^2). Subadult male lynx,

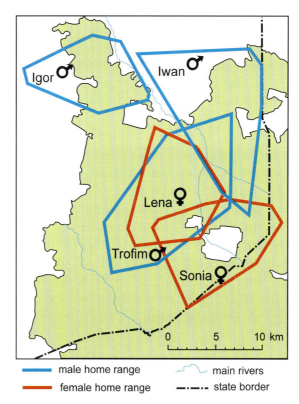

Figure 11.2. Examples of lynx home ranges studied by radio-telemetry in Białowieża Forest. (Reprinted from: *Acta Theriologica* 42: 289–312, 1997; modified.)

before coming into full maturity, roamed over areas up to 200 km^2. In contrast, home ranges of subadult females were only 80 km^2. The size of lynx home range, despite some overlapping, determines the density of their population. Only 25–35 adult lynx were estimated to exist in the whole Białowieża Forest. The main factor determining the size of lynx home ranges could be food. As roe deer are the primary prey of lynx, their densities are the reason for extensive ranging of lynx. Indeed, in Scandinavia, where roe deer populations are much scarcer than in Białowieża Forest, lynx roam up to 10-fold larger home ranges than here.

The supply of prey is not the only variable affecting home range size. Breeding females, which kill twice as many prey as males, roam over significantly smaller areas than males. Why do male lynx maintain larger territories? The explanation comes from the seasonal dynamics of home range size. Males use a relatively stable area of about 100 km^2 from April till November, but beginning in December, they start to roam widely, increasing their home range size by 90%. They maintain this large area until March, which coincides with the end of mating season. During this time, males are up to 70% more active than usual. Their daily movements increase from a "normal" average distance of 7 km to 17 km per day, in their search for females. Moreover, they travel nearly 2 km per hour during this time, which is about 0.5 km/h faster than during the rest of the year. Therefore, for males it is not food, which causes their large home ranges, but access to females.

In females, behavioural changes during the year seem to suggest that food is the limiting factor for them. From May–June, just after parturition, female home ranges decrease to 10 km^2, 10% of their normal size. During this time, a female does not go too far from the den site, as her movements are restricted by the needs of her nursing kittens. Later in summer, when the kittens' diets must be supplemented with meat, females gradually expand their ranges. In this way, they respond to the increasing food demands of the whole family.

Females also show other behavioural adjustments aimed at the successful care of offspring. From May till August, in the earliest stages of kitten development, when females have to cope with the high energy demands of lactation, they move and hunt longer than in autumn and winter, and even prolong their activity into the daylight hours. Being active on average 7.5 h per day in May–August, they cover almost 8 km, whereas later in the year they will travel just half that distance.

Thus, in the lynx population, each sex follows a different life strategy. Males make every effort to increase their chance of meeting receptive females. As a consequence, apart from prey density, the number and distribution of females influence their movements. In contrast, females appear to be mainly dependent on food accessibility as they attempt to maximize the survival of their kittens.

When a new generation of kittens becomes independent, young lynx seek their own territories. Both staying and leaving is risky for a young animal. Having decided to stay near its natal range, a subadult lynx may have poor chances of establishing its own territory and reproducing soon. Having decided to leave, it undertakes the risk of exploring unknown and potentially dangerous places.

Among six young lynx studied by radio-tracking in Białowieża Forest, three out of four males left their natal area just after separation from their mothers. They dispersed in various directions in Poland and Belarus, and covered 40–130 km routes (straight-line distance) to the sites, where they were last located (Figure 11.3). While dispersing, these lynx chose the most forested areas for travel. This emphasises the importance of this habitat for natural processes

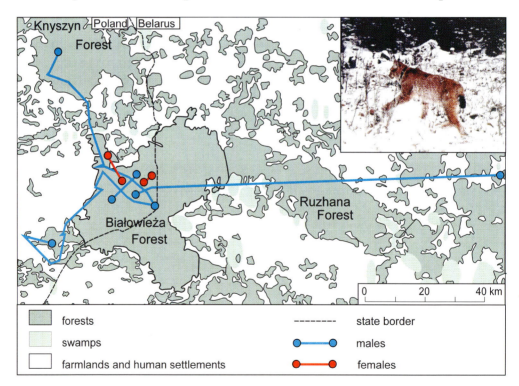

Figure 11.3. Dispersal routes of radio-collared subadult lynx born in Białowieża Forest. Broken lines connect consecutive radio-locations. Straight lines connect radio-locations in the natal area and the last location. (Reprinted from: *Acta Theriologica* 43: 391–408, 1988.) Photo by Włodzimierz Jędrzejewski.

to occur in lynx populations. The successful dispersal of individuals is the only mechanism of gene flow between neighbouring sub-populations.

The two young radio-tracked females stayed in Białowieża Forest near their natal ranges for the entire monitoring period. They seemed to confirm the prediction that females are more tolerant towards their daughters. As female behaviour is strongly governed by their investment in the kittens' survival, they probably take advantage of being familiar with food resources in the area.

Lynx in Poland

Lynx were once distributed in forested areas of the whole Palaearctic, from the Pyrenean Mountains in Europe, across Siberia to Kamchatka. At present, their range is still one of largest among wild cats, but during the last two centuries the lynx was exterminated from vast areas of Europe. Nowadays, Scandinavia, northeastern Poland and the Carpathian Mountains harbour the natural westernmost populations (Figure 11.4). In Western Europe, a few isolated, re-introduced populations have existed since the 1970's.

In Poland, the lynx has been protected since 1995. According to a recent national survey of large carnivores (1999–2001), there are

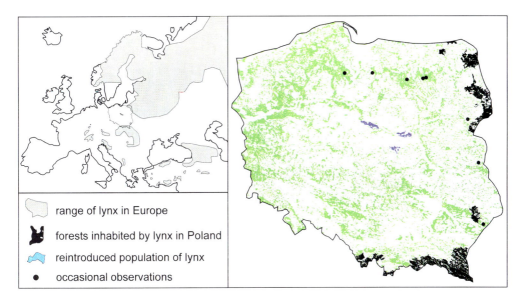

Figure 11.4. Present distribution of lynx in Europe (left) and Poland (right). (The map of lynx occurrence in Poland reprinted from: *Kosmos* 51: 491–499, 2002; modified.)

two main regions inhabited by lynx: the Carpathian Mountains and northeastern Poland (Figure 11.4). A small population has been recently established in central Poland by reintroduction. In the northeast, the cats are confined to three large woodlands: the Białowieża, Knyszyn and Augustów forests. Until the 1980's, small populations inhabited also the Pisz Forest and Napiwoda-Ramuki forests situated west of there. Lynx existed there continuously for several decades despite pressure from hunting. However, after 1995 only a few occasional observations of lynx were recorded in these forests.

Why is the lynx not able to recover and expand its range in Poland, despite its full protection? The answer is probably the fragmentation and isolation of forests inhabited by these predators. Indispensable for long-term survival of the lynx population are large and well-connected woodlands. A single forest patch, of a similar size to Białowieża Forest, which supports only a limited number of individuals (40–60) cannot ensure their survival, unless there is an exchange of individuals with other lynx populations. Successful dispersal of lynx from forest patch to forest patch will compensate for losses caused by stochastic factors and is necessary for maintaining genetic diversity over the long term. Therefore, if lynx are to survive in Poland, forest corridors should connect all actual or potentially suitable habitats for this species.

Suggested readings

Jędrzejewski W., Jędrzejewska B., Okarma H., Schmidt K., Bunevich A. N. and Miłkowski L. 1996. Population dynamics (1869–1994), demography and home ranges of the lynx in Białowieża Primeval Forest (Poland and Belarus). Ecography 19: 122–138.

Jędrzejewski W., Schmidt K., Okarma. H. and Kowalczyk R. 2002. Movement pattern and home range use by the Eurasian lynx in Białowieża Primeval Forest (Poland). Annales Zoologici Fennici 39: 29–41.

Okarma H., Jędrzejewski W., Schmidt K., Kowalczyk R. and Jędrzejewska B. 1997. Predation of Eurasian lynx on roe deer and red deer in Białowieża Primeval Forest, Poland. Acta Theriologica 42: 203–224.

Schmidt K., Jędrzejewski W. and Okarma H. 1997. Spatial organization and social relations in the Eurasian lynx population in Białowieża Primeval Forest, Poland. Acta Theriologica 42: 289–312.

Schmidt K. 1998. Maternal behaviour and juvenile dispersal in the Eurasian lynx. Acta Theriologica 43: 391–408.

Schmidt K. 1999. Variation in daily activity of the free living Eurasian lynx in Białowieża Primeval Forest, Poland. Journal of Zoology 249: 417–425.

12

Badgers
– digging after earthworms

Rafał Kowalczyk

Every night from March till October, badgers go out of their setts to slowly and systematically dodge across the forest floor in their search for earthworms. Such an evolutionary adaptation to feed on so tiny a prey is fairly unusual among large bodied carnivores, and it shapes the badger's life habits.

The badger's food

Although they are classified as carnivores, badgers are not typical hunters. With wedge-shaped bodies, short legs, and strong claws, badgers are adapted to a fossorial mode of life. When foraging, they ferret out ground vegetation and dead litter in search of earthworms. In Białowieża Forest, worms typically constitute 50% to 75% (in wet years) of food biomass consumed by badgers (Photo 12.1). The secondary foods of badgers are amphibians (30%), mammals (10%), insects (5%), and plants (5%). Interestingly, badgers frequently capture toads, which are avoided by other carnivores due to noxious secretions produced from their skin. Badgers cope with toads by eating them from below and leaving untouched the dorsal skin and parotid glands.

Earthworms are a staple food of badgers throughout the boreal and temperate regions of Europe, including habitats such as woodlands, wood-field-meadow mosaic landscapes, and pastures. But in southern Europe, where a dry and warm climate creates adverse conditions for earthworms, badgers shift their diet to vegetative foods (wild and cultivated fruits, and cereals). Even secondary food resources of badgers change in a biogeographic gradient – from small vertebrates in the boreal and temperate zones, to insects in southern Europe.

Although the gut and dentition of badgers are adapted to both plant and animal foods, a diet rich in animal protein would be more superior. Hence, what are the advantages and costs of badgers specializing on earthworms? First of all, worms are an abundant and rapidly renewable resource. In the temperate zone, the biomass of earthworms in the soil of pastures, meadows, and arable lands averages 340–1250 kg per hectare. Large species from the genus *Lumbricus*, with an individual body mass more than 4 grams, are the dominant species of earthworms. Woodlands harbour mostly small species from the genera *Allobophora* and *Dendrobaena*, with average body masses less than 1 gram. In Białowieża Forest, habitats most rich in earthworms are oak-lime-hornbeam forests. They provide over 400 kg of worms per hectare. Ash-alder wet forests offer over 300 kg per hectare, whereas mixed and coniferous forests only 50 kg per hectare. Such variation in earthworm availability among habitats influences the territory size of badgers.

Photo 12.1. Badger searching for earthworms in a pristine woodland and its main prey. Photo by Paweł Fabijański.

Earthworm availability strongly varies among seasons. In Białowieża Forest, earthworm biomass is highest in spring (on average 500 kg per hectare), followed by a five-fold decrease during summer, and then finally increasing again in autumn. In winter, earthworms are typically not available. To compensate for the summer decline of earthworms and supply their energetic needs, badgers devote a longer time to foraging, prey more on alternative foods, move further from their setts and cover larger ranges. In regions with mild, Atlantic climates, such as western Europe, earthworms are available year round and badgers stay active in all seasons. However, in central and eastern Europe, to survive long and harsh winters – when no earthworms are available – badgers stay inactive and fall into winter sleep for as long as 3–6 months every year.

Thus, badger dependence on earthworms has consequences for their densities, behaviour, home-range size and use, reproductive success, and activity patterns. Radio-telemetry studies on badgers in the well-preserved woodlands of Białowieża (from 1997 to 2001) have revealed many interesting features of their ecology.

Once trapped and anaesthetised, badgers were fitted with collars carrying radio-transmitters. These transmitters emit a continuous series of pulses, which can be detected using an antenna and a receiver tuned to the appropriate frequency. Range of signal from badger transmitters reached 800–1000 metres. The position of a badger, while active, was estimated based on the triangulation method – where the position of an animal is ascertained by the crossing of at least two bearings taken from different points and mapped. Very precise information on various aspects of badger ecology was obtained using this method.

Small families in large territories

Badgers live in social groups occupying a common sett and territory (Photo 12.2). However, individuals from a group do not cooperate in foraging or rearing young. In Białowieża Forest, size of badger groups varied from 2 to 7 individuals (both adults and cubs), with the average being 3.9. Mean litter size was 2.4 cubs (maximum of 4), however some families did not reproduce every year. Therefore, the average number of cubs per sett per year was only 1.5.

The whole Polish part of Białowieża Forest (600 km^2) harbours 22–25 social groups of badgers. Their main setts were located at a mean distance of 4 km from each other (the nearest neighbour distance). Known information on badger group size and density of

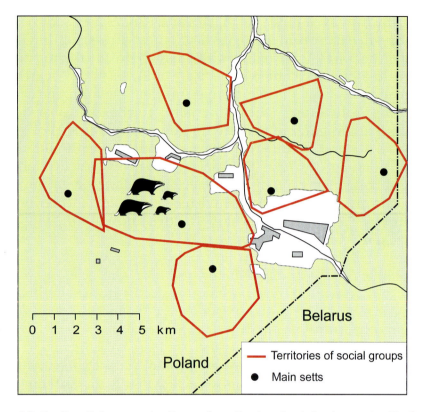

Figure 12.1. Spatial organization of radio-tracked badgers in Białowieża Primeval Forest. (Reprinted from: *Canadian Journal of Zoology* 81: 74–87, 2003; modified.)

main setts, it made possible to estimate the density of badgers living in the area. In Białowieża Forest, their density was very low and averaged 2.1 badgers per 10 km^2.

Each group of badgers occupies an exclusive territory. In Białowieża Forest, the territories are surprisingly large and cover from 8 to 25 km^2, with an average of 12.8 km^2 (Figure 12.1). Home range overlap among individual badgers from the same social group was over 70%. Adult badgers occupied ranges twice as large as those of yearlings. This is because adults have higher energetic needs due to their reproductive activity and larger body size. Adult males engage in territorial patrolling, which is especially evident during the reproductive season, while dominant females suckle cubs for almost four months. Thus, adults need to move over larger areas to supply their energetic needs.

When comparing the spatial organization of badgers living in Białowieża Forest to other European populations, one can see that territories of badgers in Białowieża Forest are surprisingly larger

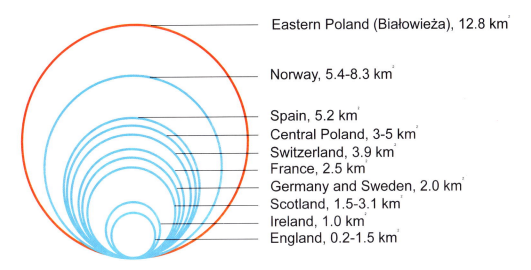

Figure 12.2. Size of badger territories from various parts of Europe.

than those observed in other regions of Europe (Figure 12.2). In some parts of the British Isles, badger groups may occupy ranges as small as 0.2 km^2, and their density may reach over 400 badgers per 10 km^2.

Why do badgers in woodlands of temperate Europe maintain so large of territories and live in such low densities? In areas where badgers feed predominantly on earthworms, their densities are largely determined by the abundance of earthworms and annual temperature. The higher the worm abundance, the higher the density of badgers. However, given a similar standing crop of food resources, badgers will attain lower densities in regions with prolonged cold seasons. The mechanism underlying this is a shorter time to exploit available resources. This indicates that in forests of central and eastern Europe, in colder climates, badgers live in low densities. Whereas in the man-made open landscapes of western Europe and the British Isles, with mild climates, badgers have much higher densities.

My sett is my castle

Badgers are inseparably connected to their setts, which are used for reproduction, winter sleep and as places of daytime rest for these night-active animals. Large and elaborate badger setts, with sandy heaps at their entrances and well-worn paths leading outwards, are inherited from generation to generation and may be occupied for over a hundred years. In Białowieża Forest, a sett which is still active today was first mentioned in historical records in 1825! When cleaning their setts, badgers often dig out skulls and other bones of their ancestors that had died in the sett.

Each group of badgers posses and utilises several shelters in their territory. However just one sett, usually the largest one which is occupied year round, plays the role of the main sett and is used for breeding and winter sleep. The other shelters are visited from spring to autumn as temporary resting sites. Interestingly in the pristine forest of Białowieża National Park, badgers also use fallen, hollow trees, mainly limes, as day-time resting sites.

Main setts have several entrances and contain a few hundred metres of underground tunnels, which cover an area of up to 250 m^2. The depth and complex structure of main setts help secure the survival of badgers during severe and long winters, in addition protecting them against wolves and lynx. From spring to autumn badgers use almost all available space within a sett. In winter, they gather in a small area within the main sett, and often huddle together.

In Białowieża Forest, most of the main badger setts are also occupied by raccoon dogs during winter. Raccoon dogs decrease their activity in the cold season, and to survive periods of food shortages, often settle in badger setts. Concurrent radio-tracking of individuals of both species wintering in the same setts have shown that badgers and their "usurpatory lodgers" use different parts of the sett, most probably to avoid contact.

The busy life of a sleepyhead

In Białowieża Forest, badgers spent over 3 months per year, from November to February, in winter sleep. This is, however, not leisure time for them, but an ecological necessity to cope with the long period when no food is available. To survive such a long time of inactivity, badgers lead busy lives in the other seasons.

From spring till autumn they are active, on average 8 hours per night. The duration of their activity varies seasonally and is inversely related to earthworm abundance. It also strongly depends on temperature. Badgers do not emerge from setts at all when the ambient temperature drops below −5°C. Such weather is not too cold for badgers, but they are simply not able to find any earthworms, which forces them to save energy. As temperatures increase, badgers become active longer and longer, and may spend as much as 15 hours searching for earthworms on very warm summer nights.

Photo 12.2. Young badgers playing near a sett. Photo by Paweł Fabijański.

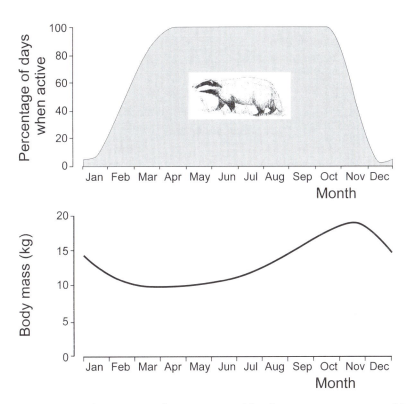

Figure 12.3. Annual pattern of activity and body mass increase of badgers in Białowieża Forest. (Reprinted from: *Journal of Biogeography* 30: 463–472, 2003; modified.)

Temperature and earthworm availability also strongly shape the annual activity pattern of badgers (Figure 12.3). From April to October, badgers go out every night, while in November they emerge from their setts only an average of 14 days. In December and January, badgers sleep in their setts, although on warmer days they may emerge and explore their surroundings. The winter sleep of badgers is not a true hibernation, but rather a torpor, because badgers lower their body temperature only slightly. This allows them to economize

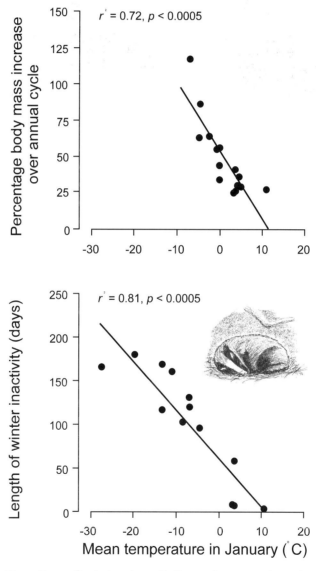

Figure 12.4. Duration of winter inactivity and percentage increase in body mass of badgers in relation to the mean temperature in January in Europe and Asia. (Reprinted from: *Journal of Biogeography* 30: 463–472, 2003.)

the loss of energy and slow down the use of their fat reserves. During warmer days, badgers may easily wake up and be active. Starting in February, badgers begin increasing their activity, and by March they are active for about 26 days. From spring to autumn, during their nocturnal foraging, badgers travel about 7 km per night (range 0.5–17.5 km).

Spring is for badgers the time of birth and mating. Young badgers are born in March, and the first 9–10 weeks of their life are spent in the sett suckling their mother. In the second half of May, cubs appear above ground for the first time, and in late June they start to follow their mother. Summer and autumn are a busy time for badgers. Females are teaching cubs how to search for food, and all badgers are feeding intensively to collect adequate fat reserves to survive the approaching winter. This is not an easy task, as earthworms are less abundant than they were in spring. Adult badgers weighing about 10 kg in spring, have to increase their body mass by almost twice to reach nearly 20 kg by late summer and autumn (Figure 12.3). They become really massive, fat and slow creatures. In autumn they also gather dry leaves, and while shuffling backwards, drag them down into their setts. Bedding is a vital insulation for badgers inside the sett tunnels in winter, when ambient temperatures may fall below –30°C.

Winter sleep and the regular fattening of badgers every autumn are observed only in cold climates. In the northernmost quarters of their distribution range (north of 60°N), badgers are active for only six months per year, and during that time they have to double their weight in order to survive the other half of the year. In the south-western and warmest, part of the badger's geographic range, their activity and body mass are rather stable year round. Length of winter sleep and percentage of body mass increase are related to winter severity (Figure 12.4). Thus, badgers have to store more fat, if they are to survive longer periods of winter sleep. The winter inactivity of badgers is an adaptation to the seasonality of food resources (availability of earthworms) rather than to cold temperatures.

The badger is a good example of the great biogeographical plasticity in physiology and ecology of a carnivore, and a great many studies were conducted on this species. However, most data comes from western Europe, and in particular Great Britain, which contain human-altered habitats. Thus far, the study conducted in Białowieża Forest has been the only research project conducted in a large and natural temperate woodland of Europe. This study has provided information on badger ecology in its pristine, ancestral habitat, as well as fresh insights, and a better understanding of their life habits.

Suggested readings

Goszczyński J., Jędrzejewska B. and Jędrzejewski W. 2000. Diet composition of badgers (*Meles meles*) in a pristine forest and rural habitats of Poland compared to other European populations. Journal of Zoology, London 250: 495–505.

Kowalczyk R., Jędrzejewska B. and Zalewski A. 2003. Annual and circadian activity patterns of badgers *Meles meles* in Białowieża Primeval Forest (E Poland) compared to other Palaearctic populations. Journal of Biogeography 30: 463–472.

Kowalczyk R., Zalewski A., Jędrzejewska B. and Jędrzejewski W. 2003. Spatial organization and demography of badgers *Meles meles* in Białowieża Forest (Poland) and the influence of earthworms on badger densities in Europe. Canadian Journal of Zoology 81: 74–87.

Kruuk H. 1989. The social badger – ecology and behaviour of a group-living carnivore (*Meles meles*). Oxford University Press, Oxford.

Neal E. and Cheeseman C. 1996. Badgers. T and AD Poyser Natural History, London.

13

The versatile pine martens

Andrzej Zalewski

The common name of the pine marten implies that this predator prefers pine forests. However, it occurs in all types of European woodlands, from boreal to Mediterranean forests. How did martens adapt to such a variety of climatic conditions, habitats, and prey types, which can vary in abundance?

Rich summer and lean winter periods

The agile bodies of pine martens are well adapted to a forest habitat. First, the surfaces of their paws are rather large in comparison to their body mass, thus acting as "snowshoes" to help them walk on snow. Secondly, they have longer and more solid, muscularly developed fore legs, which make them well adapted to arboreal life. In addition, marten claws are relatively large, with thick diameters at their bases and a great degree of curvature, similar in shape to those of squirrels. Finally, the marten's long bushy tail is important for balance when moving along branches or jumping from tree to tree (Photo 13.1).

A reflection of the morphological adaptations of martens to forest habitats is their diversified feeding habits. In Białowieża Primeval Forest, martens consume a great variety of food. When foraging on the ground, they search for rodents and frogs, and will opportunistically feed on carrion, especially on the remains of wolf and lynx kills. During the warm season, martens collect beetles, fruits such as raspberries and blueberries, and mushrooms. Their

Photo 13.1. Pine marten in Białowieża Forest. Photo by Jan Walencik.

adaptation for climbing opens to them an additional area in which to forage. In spring they investigate tree hollows in search of birds, including their eggs and nestlings. In summer and autumn, they check tree cavities to find nests of wild bees and wasps, which contain larvae and sweet honey. In autumn, martens also collect fruits and seeds from trees, such as rowanberries and hazelnuts. Despite this wide array of food, small rodents dominate the pine marten's diet. The bank vole and yellow-necked mouse constitute the most important prey species throughout the year, usually making up over 60% of total biomass consumed by martens (Figure 13.1).

While systematically searching for rodents, martens move on average 7 km per day. Although martens are good climbers, they do not travel far in the canopy. In Białowieża Forest, trees were climbed 7 times per day and distance travelled in the tree canopy was only 67 meters per day. When hunting, martens prefer areas with a local abundance of fallen logs, along which they can move swiftly. In just one day, a marten was recorded to travel along fallen logs 158 times, and to go under them 113 times. During a typical foray, martens will attack prey 32 times, but only 4–5 attacks are successful. Good sites for hunting rodents are root plates, the branches and ground beneath wind blown trees (37% of attacks), and among the roots of living trees (27% of attacks).

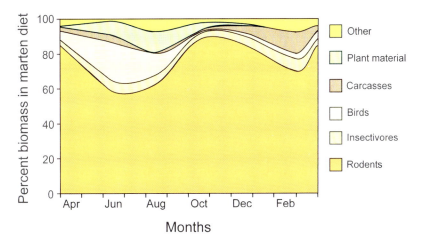

Figure 13.1. Seasonal changes in the marten diet in Białowieża National Park. Data from scat analysis 1985–1996.

The availability of forest rodents varies throughout the year. From spring to autumn, rodent numbers increase due to their high reproduction rate. This is a rich period for martens. The opposite occurs during the winter, when rodent numbers decline and deep snow cover makes hunting them more difficult. Martens then have to face a lean period. Thus, following the pattern of rodent availability, a high contribution of rodents to the marten diet is observed in autumn, when rodents are abundant, and then throughout the winter rodent shares decrease. With the arrival of spring, the consumption of rodents by martens increases again before declining during the summer. When rodent numbers decrease, martens feed on alternative prey. In winter, they feed on carrion. In summer, martens take advantage of the high availability of birds and their nests. From the great number of bird species inhabiting Białowieża Forest, martens select medium-sized-birds such as thrushes, as well as cavity nesters (woodpeckers, flycatchers, and tits)

Interestingly, during rich, warm summers, martens are active longer (13 hours on average) and move further per day (16 km on average), than during the winter period. On extremely cold days (daily temperature –20°C) martens curtail their activity to 2 hours per night, and move only 0.5 km daily. With such a short period of activity, martens need to cache enough prey to survive the next day. To save energy during cold periods, martens switch to larger prey (squirrels or large birds), and they often rest just a few metres from scavenged ungulate carcasses, feeding on them for several consecutive nights.

Annual rodent fluctuations

Over the years, numbers of forest rodents fluctuate according to cycles that follow the seed crops of oaks, hornbeams and maples. Heavy masts, occurring at 6-9-year intervals, trigger winter breeding of rodents, thus causing their numbers to soar in the following years. This will be followed by a year when rodent numbers decline heavily, before returning to moderate densities in the intervening years (Figure 13.2). As a generalist predator, pine marten, changes the composition of its diet and kill rates in response to variation in numbers of its primary prey. This is called a functional response. During outbreak years, the share of rodents (bank voles and yellow-necked mice) in marten diets increases to 90% of biomass consumed. In

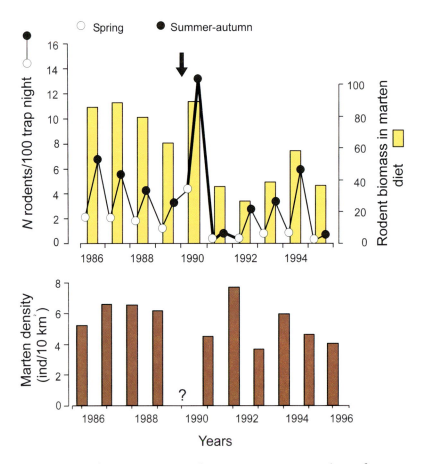

Figure 13.2. Annual variations in the spring–summer diet of pine martens in Białowieża National Park, in relation to abundance of forest rodents over a 10-year period (upper panel) and variation in pine marten density (lower panel). Arrow indicates the year with a heavy mast crop.

crash years, rodents constitute only about 40% of the food biomass consumed (Figure 13.2).

To survive the lean periods during rodent crash years, pine martens have to search for other sources of food. Birds along with their eggs and fledglings form an important alternative food in spring and summer, whereas wild fruits are important at the end of summer. In winter, the buffer foods of martens in deciduous forests are ungulate carcasses or, less preferably, shrews. When predator numbers change in response to prey fluctuations, it is called a numerical response. Since generalist predators are able to survive on buffer prey, their numbers show relatively weak numerical responses to a change in abundance of their primary prey. In rodent crash years, the density of martens was 4 individuals per 10 km^2. When rodent densities increased, the numbers of martens also increased to 8 individuals per 10 km^2 (Figure 13.2). Marten numbers are not related to the rodent population density of the current year, but to that of the previous year. This is because pine martens exhibit delayed implantation. After mating between July–August, the development of their embryos stops until February of the next year (embryonic dia-

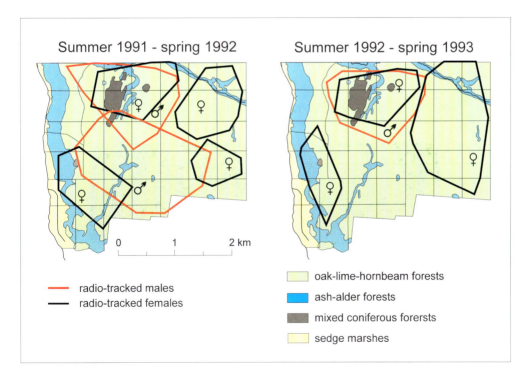

Figure 13.3. Pine marten home ranges and population spatial structure after a rodent peak year (left), and after the year of a rodent crash (right). (Reprinted from: *Annales Zoologici Fennici* 32: 131–144, 1995; modified.)

pause), and the litter is born in March or April. This is why marten numerical responses to variation in rodent densities have a one--year lag.

Due to relatively small fluctuations in pine marten density, their spacing pattern and home range sizes are quite stable among years (Figure 13.3). Pine martens are solitary predators but there is generally a notable overlap of home ranges between the sexes (20% on average). However, females always exclude other females, and males generally exclude other males from their ranges. In Białowieża National Park, the mean home range of males covered 2.6 km^2 (range: 1.0–4.0 km^2) and that of females covered 1.4 km^2 (0.5–2.6 km^2). In years with a very low abundance of rodents, the possibility of encounters between martens is low. Therefore, martens markedly change how they use their home ranges. Their daily routes become longer (average 6.5 km) and daily ranges become bigger (75 ha). In years of high rodent densities, martens cover on average 4.1 km daily, and their daily ranges embrace 43 ha. Thus, thanks to their versatile feeding habits, martens can overcome fluctuating rodent numbers with relatively small changes in their own numbers and spatial structure.

Life gets harder towards the north

In large parts of the pine marten's geographical range, winters are severe, snow cover is deep and the difference between the warmest

Photo 13. 2. Pine marten in winter. Photo by Jan Walencik.

and coldest months can be up to 70°C (Photo 13.2). Furthermore, different geographical zones, from the Mediterranean to boreal forests, vary in the type of food resources available to martens. Because winter is the most difficult period for martens to survive, especially in the north, it is interesting to see how large-scale geographic variations affect their winter diet. Within their geographical range, martens hunt prey ranging in weight from as much as 4 kg (hares) down to as little as 3 g (such as shrews). Throughout Europe, from 35 to 70°N, pine martens hunt mainly small mammals (Figure 13.4), which are the main winter food source of martens in the temperate zone. However, the importance of small mammals becomes smaller at both lower and higher latitudes. The contribution of birds and medium--size mammals (squirrels and hares) to marten diets increases from south to north (Figure 13.4). In boreal forests, martens hunt for larger birds such as black and willow grouse, hazel hens, and capercaillies. Plant material (rowanberries, carob fruit, rose hips as well as citrus and figs) is the primary food of pine martens in southern Europe, and its proportion in their diet decreases towards the north.

As rodent densities are positively correlated with net productivity of ground vegetation, which decline from temperate deciduous and mixed forests to boreal forests, the pine marten's food niche and diet breadth is wider in northern than in southern Europe. Furthermore, because it takes more time to search for scarcer prey, pine martens move longer distances per day in northern Europe (on average, 8.1 km/day at 70°N) than in the south (2.5 km at 40°N).

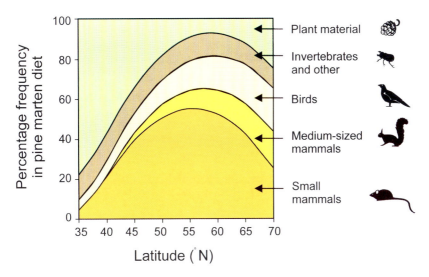

Figure 13.4. Latitudinal variation in the winter diet of pine martens in Europe based on empirical data from 43 field studies.

Pine martens do not follow Bergman's rule. This means smaller martens inhabit northern Europe, whereas larger ones live in the south. This phenomenon was previously explained by the need for martens to adapt to hunting larger prey in southern Europe. However, martens generally hunt bigger prey in the northern regions than in the south. In effect, in the south, larger martens eat smaller prey, whereas in the north, smaller martens hunt bigger prey. Smaller individuals have lower food requirements. If they successfully hunt big prey they, can stay longer in insulated resting sites and minimize energy expenditures at lower temperatures. Therefore, the adaptation to cold climates involved changes in marten behaviour rather than increases in their body size. Once again, versatile feeding habits are the key adaptation of martens to severe northern conditions.

Despite all these amazing adaptations, the pine marten cannot survive the destruction of its vital habitat: the forest. Wherever woodlands shrink, martens are threatened by extinction. Primeval forests such as Białowieża are not only a great refuge for martens, but also a unique place to study their life habits.

Suggested reading

Jędrzejewski W., Zalewski A. and Jędrzejewska B. 1993. Foraging by pine marten *Martes martes* in relation to food resources in Białowieża National Park, Poland. Acta Theriologica 38: 405–426.

Zalewski A., Jędrzejewski W. and Jędrzejewska B. 1995. Pine marten home ranges, numbers and predation on vertebrates in a deciduous forest (Białowieża National Park, Poland). Annales Zoologici Fennici 32: 131–144.

Zalewski A. 2000. Factors affecting the duration of activity by pine martens (*Martes martes*) in the Białowieża National Park, Poland. Journal of Zoology, London 251: 439–447.

Zalewski A. 2004. Geographical and seasonal variation in food habits and prey size of the European pine marten *Martes martes*. [In: Martens and fishers (*Martes*) in human-altered environments: An international perspective. D. J. Harrison, A. K. Fuller and G. Proulx, eds]. Kluwer Academic Publishers, Norwell, Massachusetts, USA.

Zalewski A., Jędrzejewski W. and Jędrzejewska B. 2004. Mobility and home range use by pine martens *Martes martes* in a Poland's primeval forest. Ecoscience 11: 113–122.

14

Weasel
– hard life of a small predator

Karol Zub

'Is this a weasel? It's so small! I thought it was much bigger!' These are the usual comments of people, who see a weasel for the first time. The smallest mammalian carnivore in the world, the weasel is like a fine-tuned instrument perfectly adapted to hunt rodents, but also very sensitive to changes in their abundance.

Advantages and costs of small body size

Weasels are the smallest mammalian carnivores in the world. Thin and long bodies enable them to follow rodents inside their shelters. Thus, weasels occur in nearly all environments inhabited by rodents, from semi-deserts to tundra, and in both Eurasia and North America. Specialised hunting skills make weasels efficient predators, but at the same time make them highly vulnerable.

The small body of a weasel loses heat very fast, mainly due to its high surface to volume ratio. Moreover, the need to move through narrow passages affects the body's insulation, as the fur must be relatively short and fat reserves limited. In effect, the costs of thermoregulation in weasels are much higher than in more normally shaped mammals of the same weight. In response to this, weasels developed behavioural adaptations to survive seasonally harsh conditions of the temperate and boreal zones. For example, weasels avoid excessive energy expenditures by resting inside the insulated nests of their prey, which they often line with rodent fur. During the warm season

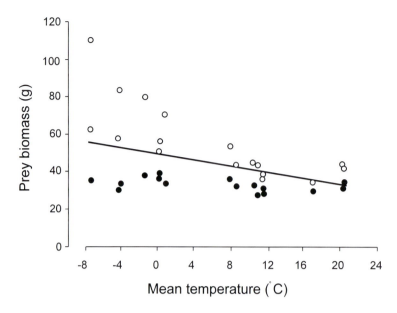

Figure 14.1. Effect of seasonal changes in temperature on weasel hunting rates – results of an experiment in outdoor enclosures. Solid circles represent mean daily consumption by weasels. Open circles are mean prey amount captured per day with hunting. The solid line designates the predicted killing rate (daily consumption in relation to hunting days). Surplus killings clearly increased with cold temperatures. (Reprinted from: *Acta Theriologica* 34: 347–359, 1989.)

Photo 14.1. Radio-collared male weasel coming out of a trap. Photo by Karol Zub.

weasels capture only the number of prey needed to satisfy their daily energy requirements, but during cold periods they begin hunting in surplus and store food in shelters (Figure 14.1). Enclosure experiments showed that most surplus killings occurred in days with temperatures from 5°C to −5°C. The kill rate was then about 3 rodents per day (maximum 12 voles per day), whereas on days with the mean daily temperature above 5°C, weasels killed on average 2 rodents per day (maximum 5).

In Białowieża Forest, during summer, radio-tracked weasels Photo 14.1) were active almost 6 hours per day. In winter, they shortened their activity to a mere 2 hours per day. In all seasons, weasels clearly showed diurnal activity, with a peak around 10.00–13.00 hours (Figure 14.2).

Although the maximum age of weasels in captivity can exceed 3 years, in the wild they live on average less than 1 year. Consequently, they attempt to reproduce even when prey is scarce. Under such

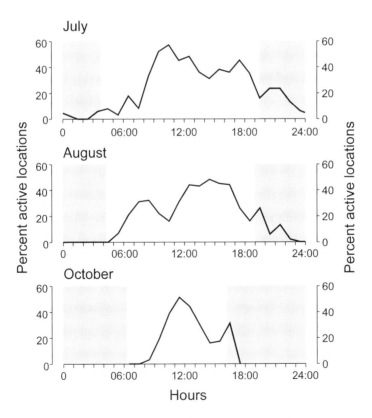

Figure 14.2. Daily activity rhythms of weasels in Białowieża National Park. Shaded bars denote night hours. Solid lines mark percentage of locations when radio-collared weasels were found active outside their dens. (Reprinted from: *Annales Zoologici Fennici* 37: 161–168, 2000; modified.)

unfavourable conditions, mortality of young before they are weaned is very high. Reproductive success of weasels is positively correlated with the abundance of rodents, and full productivity potential can be achieved only at rodent peaks. During this time, female weasels can have more than one litter per year with 5–6 young in a litter. Furthermore, female weasels mature at the age of 3 months, and can produce young within the same year they were born.

The advantages and costs of small body size also can be considered in relation to the sexes. Females raise their young alone, so they tend to be smaller and to minimize energy requirements. A smaller size enables them to penetrate all kinds of rodent shelters and increase their hunting efficiency. This is particularly important; as females have higher energy demands during lactation, and later, with growing food requirements of juveniles before weaning.

Males are polygynous and attempt to maximize their number of matings. The bigger size of males enables them to explore larger areas in search of receptive females. In terms of competing for mates, larger males have the advantage over smaller ones. In years of favourable food conditions (e.g. rodent peak years) males grew bigger and heavier, but when food supplies were poor they stopped growing earlier to allocate energy for reproduction. Therefore, the degree of sexual dimorphism in weasels can also depend on prey availability.

Weasels and forests rodents

Because weasels are highly specialised in hunting rodents (Photo 14.2), we can expect their diets to change little in response to rodent fluctuations. Instead, weasels follow the ups and downs of rodent densities with changes in their own numbers. In the pristine deciduous forests of Białowieża National Park, population dynamics of rodents are driven by the seed crops of oak and hornbeam, and are characterised by 2 year outbreaks and crashes, followed by 4–6 years of moderate densities (see Chapter 16). In addition to long-term fluctuations, these rodents show seasonal changes in abundance. The lowest numbers are observed in spring. Rodents reproduce during summer and their densities peak in late summer or autumn. The weasel population also is characterised by a similar increase in number from spring (April) to mid-summer (July/August), when it reaches the average density of 4–5 individuals per 1 km^2 (Figure 14.3). Beginning in late summer, weasels always decline in numbers, and their early winter (December) density averages 3 individuals per 1 km^2. Winter mortality, though variable, usually exceeds 60%.

In response to an outbreak of forest rodents, weasels reproduce and survive better, and from July–August attain very high densities (over 10 individuals per 1 km^2). However, in late summer, regardless that prey is still superabundant, weasel numbers start to decline. By September, their abundance is only slightly higher than those recorded in summers with moderate numbers of rodents. In the summer of a rodent crash year, fewer than 2 weasels per 1 km^2 can be found in the forest. Worse still, in the year following a rodent crash, weasels are very scarce (Figure 14.3).

The population growth of weasels is constrained by climatic factors, their own spacing behaviour, and predation. Because weasels do not breed in winter, they respond numerically to rodent fluctuations only in spring and summer. During favourable food conditions, their numbers can increase 5-fold from spring till the end of summer, and litter sizes can increase up to 8 young. In autumn, irrespective of rodent abundance, the weasel population declines, mainly due to dispersal of young and predation. The significant feature of weasel population dynamics, in pristine deciduous forests (Photo 14.3), is the high correlation between weasel and rodent numbers, and that the numerical response of weasels has no time lag.

Weasels are solitary and territorial. The sizes of their home ranges vary with rodent fluctuations. The average home range size of a radio-collared male weasel, during a rodent outbreak, was about

Photo 14.2. Radio-collared male weasel in Białowieża National Park. Photo by Karol Zub.

24 ha, whereas when rodent numbers crashed it covered 167 ha, being seven times larger (Figure 14.4). In the summer of a rodent outbreak year, the presence of several other weasels was recorded within home ranges of radio-collared males. During the year of a rodent crash no other weasels were recorded in the home ranges of any radio-tracked males.

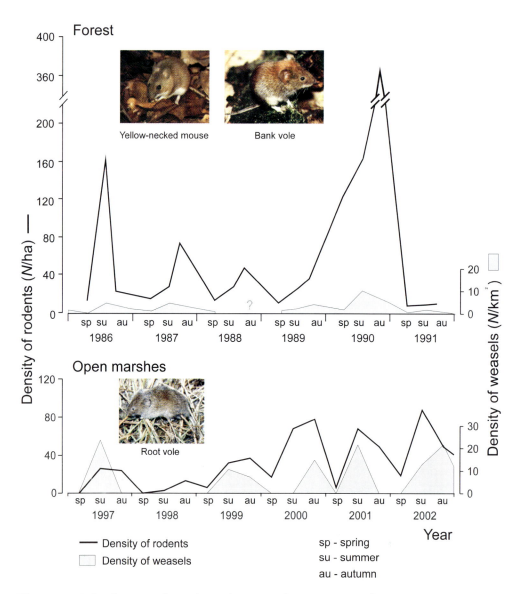

Figure 14.3. Seasonal and multiannual variation of rodent and weasel densities in the forests of Białowieża National Park (top) and neighbouring sedge meadows in the Narewka river valley (bottom). Photos by Sławomir Wąsik.

Weasels and voles in riverside marshes

The ancestors of modern weasels appeared during the late Pliocene, when extensive open grasslands replaced forests, due to the periodical cooling of the climate. Weasels evolved to exploit a new predator niche, and they are still at home in open areas (Photo 14.3). Riverside marshes are very good habitats for weasels for several reasons. First of all, the soil is usually too wet for rodents to establish deep, underground tunnels. Thus, rodents that spend most of their time in nests and runways above ground are more susceptible to weasel predation. Moreover, dense vegetation provides weasels safety from avian predators, and offers shelter from cold, particularly when covered with snow.

Photo 14.3. Weasel habitats in Białowieża Forest: forests of Białowieża National Park – a view from a weasel's perspective (top), and open marshes and meadows in the Narewka river valley (bottom). Photos by Karol Zub.

Root voles dominate the rodent community in river valleys of Białowieża Forest (see Chapter 17). Whereas drier parts of the river valley, as well as neighbouring meadows and fields, are inhabited mainly by common and field voles. Population dynamics of voles in riverside marshes are characterised by 3 to 4-yr cycles, but still with substantial seasonal variations in their densities. Again, weasels respond to both seasonal and yearly changes in vole densities, and reach their highest number in late summer and early autumn. Weasel densities in river valleys are higher than those in the forest, and average nearly 10 individuals per 1 km^2. During the peak phase, the density of weasels can reach over 15 individuals per 1 km^2, but in the low phase, weasels disappeared from the river valley.

Because the densities of weasels are higher in riverside marshes than in the forest, their home ranges are smaller. The average home range size was 18 hectares for males and 6 hectares for females. During low vole densities, male home ranges can increase up to 30 ha, but they are still much smaller than those found in the forests of Białowieża National Park (Figure 14.4).

Among specialist mammalian predators, the weasel is the first likely candidate to be responsible for cyclic fluctuations in rodents. Population cycles remain one of the puzzles and unresolved issues of ecology. Although both specialist and generalist predators hunt rodents, only specialist mammalian predators can potentially cause cyclic fluctuations in prey abundance. The main idea of this hypothesis is that the delayed numerical response of weasels causes an inverse density-dependent mortality of voles, and drives the cycles. In other words, weasels are still numerous, when rodents become scarce, and continue to hunt the few remaining voles. During the increasing phase of a rodent cycle, the number of weasels is predicted to be very low and their predation rather weak. However, empirical studies performed in Białowieża Forest, both in the forests and riverside marshes, showed that weasel numerical responses to changes in prey abundance were immediate, with no time lag. Moreover, the impact of weasels on rodents was heavier during the reproductive season of both prey and predator than in winter and early spring, when weasels do not reproduce. Thus, the numerical response of weasels and their heaviest impact on rodents takes place from summer-autumn, when rodents reproduce at a rate far beyond mortality caused by predation. From these observations we can conclude that weasel predation is neither sufficient nor necessary to initiate and drive the cyclic fluctuations of small rodents.

In spite of several decades of research on weasels, there are still unanswered questions about this species. One of the most intriguing issues is the variation in body size of weasels. The smallest animals are found in the far eastern and northern part of their geographic range, and they become larger towards the west and south, thus opposite to the predictions of Bergman's Rule. In Białowieża Forest, differences in weasel body size exist even between forest and non-forest habitats. Animals living in sedge meadows in the river valleys are larger than those inhabiting woodlands, and the difference is significant both in male and female weasels. Are prey species (their number and accessibility associated with type of environment) the main factor influencing body size of weasels? Is the gene flow in weasel populations between meadow and forest habitats reduced? Further genetic studies and observations of radio-tracked animals will tackle these questions.

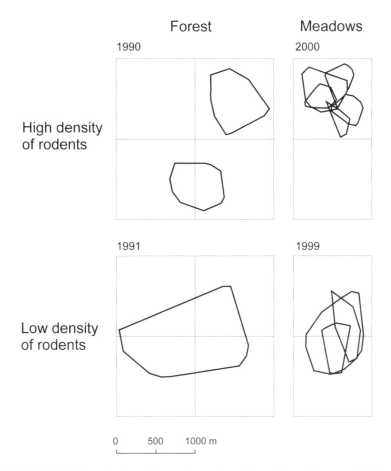

Figure 14.4. Variation in territory size of radio-collared weasels in relation to prey densities in the forests and riverside marshes of Białowieża Forest.

Suggested readings

Brown J. H. and Lasiewski R. C. 1972. Metabolism of weasel: the cost of being long and thin. Ecology 53: 939–943.

Hanski I., Hansson L. and Henttonen H. 1991. Specialist predators, generalist predators and the microtine rodent cycle. Journal of Animal Ecology 60: 353–367.

Jędrzejewska B. and Jędrzejewski W. 1989. Seasonal surplus killing as hunting strategy of the weasel *Mustela nivalis* – test of hypothesis. Acta Theriologica 34: 347–359.

Jędrzejewski W., Jędrzejewska B. and Szymura L. 1995. Weasel population response, home range, and predation on rodents in a deciduous forest in Poland. Ecology 76: 179–195.

Jędrzejewski W., Jędrzejewska B., Zub K. and Nowakowski W. K. 2000. Activity patterns of radio-tracked weasels *Mustela nivalis* in Białowieża National Park (E Poland). Annales Zoologici Fennici 37: 161–168.

15

Bats in trees

Ireneusz Ruczyński

In May, after a few hundred kilometres of journey, Leisler's bats arrive in Białowieża Primeval Forest to rear their young. Old-growth forests are rich in natural cavities, and here bats seek roosts that will protect females and their babies from cold temperatures and predators. As early as August, Leisler's bats leave the forest and head south to their mating and wintering quarters.

A long life with many journeys

Although its geographical range covers large parts of Europe, Asia, and North Africa, the Leisler's bat is a rare and little known species. In Białowieża Primeval Forest, Leisler's bats (Photo 15.1), which are forest dwellers and live in tree cavities, find excellent habitats. However, they stay here only 4–5 months per year. Adult females appear in the forest in early May. Young are born in mid-June, after 45–50 days of pregnancy. Already by early August, adult females begin their southerly migration, whereas juveniles may stay until the end of August.

Curiously enough, adult males have not been observed in Białowieża Forest thus far. Also, in other northern regions, such as Voronezh in Russia, males occur sporadically (one male per 200 females), whereas in southern Europe (Greece, France, and Macedonia), males dominate in populations of Leisler's bats. Having mated with females in their southern quarters, male bats need not undertake the risk and effort of migration and do not participate in the rearing of young.

Photo 15.1. Leisler's bats. Photos by Robert Mysłajek.

In late summer, females from Białowieża Forest migrate 300–500 km either to the south or southwest. The longest recorded movement – from Germany to Spain – covered 1,568 km. In central Europe, the mating season lasts from early August till mid-September. Males keep transient harems of one to six (sometimes up to 12) females. After copulation, females store sperm in their uterus and oviducts through the winter, and fertilisation takes place several months later – in spring.

From September till March or mid-April, Leisler's bats hibernate in tree cavities, buildings, or rock crevices. In April, another short mating period can be observed just before adult females migrate to northern regions. Because Leisler's bats live up to 9 years, these journeys over a female's life can total a few thousands kilometres.

Colonies in the forest

In Białowieża Forest, a single breeding colony of Leisler's bats was found some 50 years ago. During the following decades further investigations by traditional methods did not yield any results. It was radio-telemetry techniques first applied in 1998, that successfully located the colonies of these bats in the forest. To accomplish this, Leisler's bats were caught in mist-nets set over the rivers, and tiny radio transmitters (0.5–0.7 g) were attached with surgical adhesive to their backs. This made it possible to find their roosts in cavities of old trees.

Breeding colonies in cavities comprise of females and juveniles. Mixed colonies of Leisler's bats and noctules are quite common. Starting in mid-July, they form about 30% of all colonies. In early summer, the mean number of bats emerging at dusk from a roost ranged from 14 to 20 individuals. In late July, when juveniles began to fly, the mean number of bats emerging from a roost increased to 26 individuals. The largest colony – 97 individuals emerging from a cavity – was observed on 24th of July, 1999. By gathering in one roost, bats keep warm and conserve energy during cold days. This is crucial for the development of embryos and juveniles, especially during periods of cool, windy, and rainy weather.

How do Leisler's bats utilise their roosts? Trees with roost cavities were located at distances of 0.5 to 6 km (mean 2 km) from points of capture (Figure 15.1). Colonies used several roosts distri-

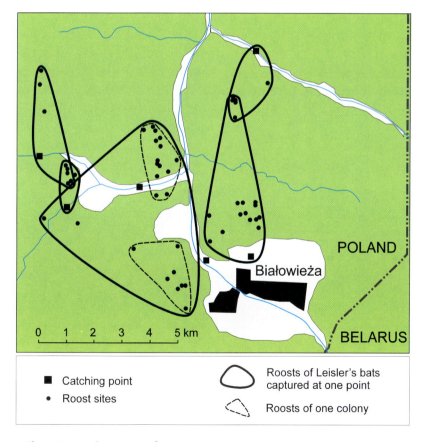

Figure 15.1. Distribution of roost trees occupied by colonies of Leisler's bats in Białowieża Forest from 1998–2000.

buted over an area of 2 km^2, moving from one roost to another at 1 to 7-day intervals. These subsequently occupied roosts were located at a mean distance of 0.7 km from each other. Such frequent changes probably help bats to avoid parasites and predators. Usually, the whole colony shifts from one roost to another during one night. This suggests that Leisler's bats have a good communication system. When juveniles are small and unable to fly, their mothers transport them from one roost to another. Occasionally, a colony will split into a few subgroups, which simultaneously use more than one tree. During summer, Leisler's bats often return to previously used roost trees. Moreover, they may return to the same cavity year after year. Out of 9 roosts utilised in 1998, at least 3 were used again in summer 1999. In Białowieża Forest, some cavities in trees were occupied by Leisler's bats for 3 years.

When pregnant, females spent 90% of the whole day and night in roosts (Figure 15.2). They started emerging a few minutes after sunset, and their aerial foraging for insects lasted about 75 minutes. During the night they flew back to the roost 1–3 times. Their total activity outside the shelter took, on average, 2 hours and 10 minutes. At the latest, bats returned from foraging shortly before sunrise (Figure 15.2). After parturition, female activity patterns changed. Lactating females emerged earlier, about 5–30 minutes before sunset, and they spent up to 3 hours and 10 minutes per

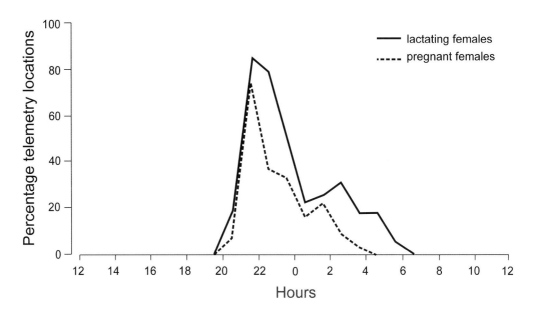

Figure 15.2. Pattern of daily activity of female Leisler's bats in summer, in relation to their reproductive status.

night hunting. They returned to the roost up to 7 times per night to feed their young.

Furthermore, ambient temperature influenced the duration of bat activity. When it was fairly cool (15–18°C), they spent more time in roosts. As temperatures increased, bats prolonged their activity. However, when the mean ambient temperature exceeded 24°C, bats stayed longer in their cavities.

Warm and safe cavities

The natural old-growth forest of Białowieża National Park provides an unusual diversity and number of potential roosts for Leisler's bats (Photo 15.2). In standing (living or dead) trees with natural cracks and woodpecker holes, bats can find good shelters. Leisler's bats

Photo 15.2. Old-growth stands of Białowieża National Park – optimal habitat for forest bats. Photos by Karol Zub and Ireneusz Ruczyński.

were most often located in oak trees (58% of occupied trees), less often in ash (26%), and rarely in alder, maple, hornbeam, pine, and lime trees. Comparison of roost trees and those available in the surrounding stands showed that bats strongly preferred oak, and less so ash, whereas they clearly avoided hornbeam and spruce trees. Trees chosen by Leisler's bats for roosts were old and large. Their diameter at breast height averaged 84 cm, whereas the mean for available trees was 40 cm. Most of the roost trees were over 160 years old.

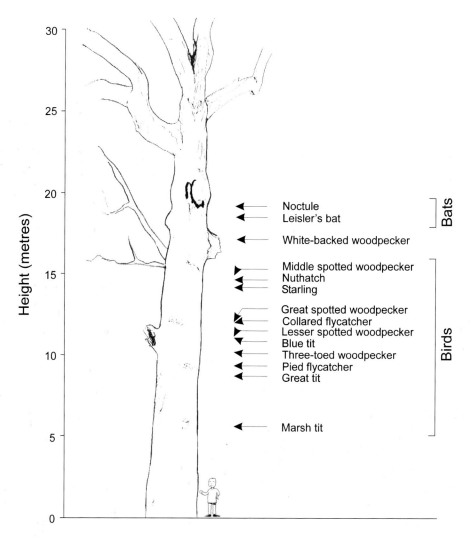

Figure 15.3. The average height of roosts used by Leisler's bats and noctules, compared to the mean height of cavity-nesting birds in Białowieża Forest. Drawing of a tree by C. Duriez.

Leisler's bats also preferred dying trees (80% of all occupied trees). Less often they used dead (14%) and healthy trees (6%). To find out which features of a cavity make it most attractive for Leisler's bats, roost cavities were compared with random holes, not occupied by bats. Several interesting differences were found. Roost cavities had smaller entrances (maximum width 6 cm) and narrower inner spaces than random holes. In addition, canopies surrounding roost cavities were not as dense. Interestingly, the shortest distance from the entrance to the furthest point inside the cavity, the so-called "safety distance" was nearly twice as long in roost cavities as those in random holes. The safety distance approximates how far a pine marten or other predator could penetrate the cavity without going in.

The average height of roost cavities was 18 metres, whereas random holes (mean height 8 m) and holes of cavity-nesting birds were located markedly lower (Figure 15.3). Thermal regime in the forest explains the very high location of bat roosts. In the natural,

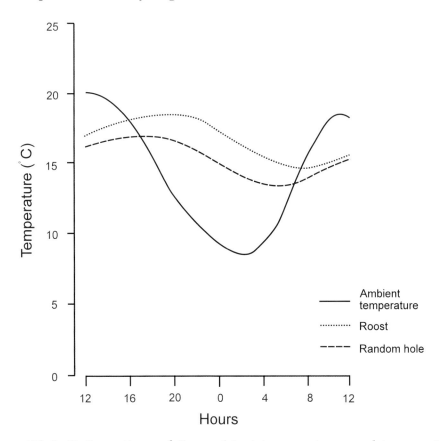

Figure 15.4. Daily pattern of the ambient temperature, and temperatures inside a roost cavity (previously used by bats) and a random hole (based on measurements in May–July, 2002).

multilayered stands of Białowieża Forest, vegetation is denser in the lower than in the upper layers. Measurements of ambient temperatures conducted from June–July, at a height of 10, 20, and 30 m, showed that the highest daily temperatures were recorded at 30 m, and the lowest at 10 m, the difference being nearly 3°C. As the temperature measured inside hollow trees correlated with the ambient temperature (Figure 15.4), cavities located higher up were truly warmer than lower ones. Furthermore, there was a notable temperature difference between roosts and random holes, especially during the night. At this time, ambient temperature as well as the temperature inside the holes markedly declined, but remained the highest in roost cavities. This indicates that Leisler's bats are experts in selecting warm roosts, an adaptation that can be crucial for survival of their young, when females are out foraging.

Finally, the study on colonies of Leisler's bats, which live and rear their young in Białowieża Forest, shows that conservation of old-growth woodlands, with old, large and dying trees, is essential for the survival of forest bat species. Commercial forests, with their rejuvenated stands and simplified structure, offer very poor, if any, habitats and roost sites for forest bats. As the Leisler's bat rarely uses nest boxes, its populations can only be protected by more conservation-oriented forest management, where dead and dying trees, as well as patches of old stands with oaks are retained.

Suggested readings

Altringham J. D. 1996. Bats: biology and behaviour. Oxford University Press, Oxford, New York, Tokyo: 1–262.

Barclay M. R. and Harder L. D. 2003. Life Histories of bats: Life in the slow lane. [In: Bat ecology. T. H. Kunz and M. B. Fenton, ed.]. The University of Chicago Press, Chicago and London: 209–253.

Bogdanowicz W. and Ruprecht A. L. 2004. *Nyctalus leisleri* (Kuhl, 1817) – Kleinabendsegler. [In: Handbuch der Säugetiere Europas, Bd. 4/II. F. Krapp, ed.]. Aula-Verlag, Wiebelsheim: 717-756.

Kunz T. H. 2003. Ecology of cavity and foliage roosting bats. [In: Bat ecology. T. H. Kunz and M. B. Fenton, ed.]. The University of Chicago Press, Chicago and London: 1–89.

Ruczyński I. and Ruczyńska I. 2000. Roosting sites of Leisler's bat *Nyctalus leisleri* in Białowieża Forest – preliminary results. Myotis 37: 55–60.

16

Seed crops and forest rodents

**Bogumiła Jędrzejewska, Zdzisław Pucek
and Włodzimierz Jędrzejewski**

In Białowieża Forest, huge, old oaks shed enormous quantities of seeds at 6 to 9-year intervals. Small forest rodents will immediately begin feeding on fallen acorns, triggering a long chain of ecological events. This includes an outbreak and consecutive crash in rodent numbers, which coincide with a periods of feasting and fasting for their predators, and elevated predation on forest-nesting birds. Interestingly, these mast-driven waves of rodent fluctuations occur in synchrony throughout Europe, wherever ancient oak forests are still growing.

Seeds and rodents

European deciduous and mixed forests offer two major food resources for small rodents: green, herbaceous vegetation on the forest floor, and seeds of trees. Shaded by dense canopies of broad-leaved trees, plant cover on the ground is meager: on average 500 kg of dry weight per hectare, that is, only one-fifth of that found in open meadows in the same climatic zone. It is also strongly seasonal, with peak development and blossoming in spring and early summer, and very scanty green plants in winter.

Seeds of trees fall in autumn and winter, and their crop is extremely variable, from 0 to over 5 tons per hectare. Among the over dozen species of European forest trees, five produce seeds that are eagerly consumed and highly preferred by bank voles and yellow--necked mice: oak, beech, lime, hornbeam and maple. In Białowieża

Forest, the oak-lime-hornbeam forest (with the common or English oak and the small-leaved lime) is the dominate association among deciduous woods. Interestingly, oak, hornbeam, and Norway maple trees growing together in such forests exhibit highly synchronised fruiting patterns. Heavy crops of seeds occur at 6 to 9-year intervals (mean 7.7 years). During the intervening years, seed crops are small and irregular, and they usually fail to occur in years following the mast. In over 30 years, only once did the oak crop lag one year behind that of hornbeams (Figure 16.1).

In the woodlands of Białowieża, the community of forest rodents is dominated by bank voles and yellow-necked mice (Photo 16.1), which together make up 80% of all rodents. Bank voles feed on green plants and supplement their diet with seeds, fruit, and invertebrates. The mice are granivorous, as they live on tree seeds but also eat some green vegetation and invertebrates. Seeds of trees, particularly oak, hornbeam, and maple are not only an important food resource for both species, but are the main factor shaping annual variations in their densities.

Over 30-years of data on bank vole and yellow-necked mouse numbers in the oak-lime-hornbeam forests of Białowieża National Park, showed rodent population dynamics to be strongly mast--dependent (Figure 16.1). These dynamics were characterized by an outbreak (triggered by a heavy seed crop), followed by a crash in their numbers, separated by 4–7 years of moderate rodent numbers. In years with small or failed seed crops, rodent numbers are lowest in spring (densities 6–15 individuals/ha). Then, throughout the summer they increase due to breeding and reach 10–160 individuals/ha by autumn. Reproduction ceases in autumn, and high winter mortality again leads to low numbers of rodents the following spring. Annual

Photo 16.1. Bank vole (left) and yellow-necked mouse (right). Photos by Sławomir Wąsik.

changes in rodent numbers are linked to the biomass of herbaceous vegetation on the forest floor. In years when oak and hornbeam trees shed masses of seeds in autumn and winter, the extra food improves winter survival of voles and mice and can even cause their winter breeding. During the following spring and summer, rodents make use of both stored seeds and fresh vegetation, and continue to increase in numbers. As a result, very high densities (up to 300 rodents per hectare) are recorded in autumn, the year after a heavy seed fall. The outbreak lasts shortly, and already in winter a dramatic decline takes place and is often followed by a one year crash. Conducive to this is the fact that trees hardly produce any seeds in a year following the mast. Notable deviations from this scheme were the years 1996 and 1997, when the outbreak lasted 2 years due to the fact that a heavy oak crop lagged one year behind the hornbeam crop (Figure 16.1).

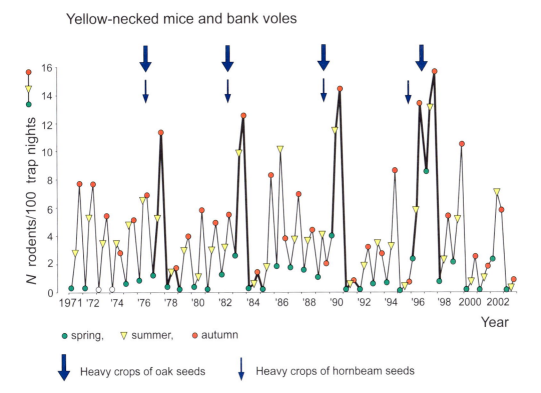

Figure 16.1. Long-term dynamics of the combined numbers of bank voles and yellow-necked mice in Białowieża National Park in relation to heavy seed crops of oaks and hornbeams. Thick line indicates outbreak and crash years, thin lines indicates years of moderate densities. (Reprinted from: *Polish Journal of Ecology* 48, Suppl.: 163–177, 2000; modified.)

A link in the food chain

Bank voles and yellow-necked mice are part of a longer food chain that comprises seeds, rodents, and predators. Abundant seeds mean a feast for rodents. Similarly, half a year later, the ensuing outbreak of rodents leads to a feast for their predators. Weasels, pine martens, and tawny owls (Photo 16.2) respond to rodent abundance by increasing their predation on them. Hence, bank voles and yellow--necked mice constitute up to 90% of their consumed food biomass in years of outbreaks. These predators try to allocate this extra energy intake towards producing more young. Weasels are the most successful at this, capable of bringing up to three litters in one spring-summer season, an unusual feat among carnivores (see Chapter 14). Less flexible in this respect are tawny owls, which invariably can only have one litter per year, with a maximum number of 5 eggs in a clutch. The least fortunate seem to be pine martens,

Photo 16.2. Tawny owl – the main predator of rodents in Białowieża Forest. Photo by Sławomir Wąsik.

which were equipped by evolution with delayed implantation. This adaptation prolongs the breeding cycle of martens and causes a higher number of young to be born with a one-year lag, falling within the year of a rodent crash. Instead of enjoying the abundance of prey, they have to cope with an extreme paucity of rodents (see Chapter 13).

Unlike the peaks of cyclic rodents in boreal and arctic zones, mast-dependent outbreaks of rodents in temperate forests do not attract nomadic raptors. In the temperate forest zone there are no birds of prey similar in their life habits to the snowy owl, hawk owl, Tengmalm's owl, and rough-legged buzzard in the north. Perhaps the only such species in the temperate zone is the long-eared owl, a migratory bird feeding on *Microtus* voles in open habitats. In years of forest rodent outbreaks, long-eared owls can breed deep in the forest interior.

A population crash of bank voles and yellow-necked mice that occurs one year after an outbreak is a real challenge for all predators. Specialists, such as weasels, are not capable of compensating for this scarcity of rodents by hunting other prey. They die or emigrate to other habitats. Weasel densities differ by up to 5-fold between rodent outbreak and crash years. Tawny owls shift to hunting more birds, frogs, and shrews, but they fail to rear young, and resident populations decline by 30%. Pine martens also strive to compensate for the lack of rodents by hunting more birds and shrews, consuming more fruit and scavenging on ungulate carrion. They too suffer a marked decline in numbers, but due to delayed implantation this decline occurs one year after the rodent crash.

Although nearly all carnivores and birds of prey occasionally capture forest rodents, over 80% of total predation is exerted by only three species: the tawny owl, weasel, and pine marten. In spring and summer, predators harvest rodents during their intense breeding season, when numbers of rodents grow. Predators consume 20–40% of total rodent numbers in years of moderate and outbreak densities, and up to 80% in a rodent crash year. Therefore, only in crash years are predators effective in halting the population growth of rodents.

In autumn and winter seasons, when rodents – except during mast years – generally declined due to a scarcity of winter food, predation is the major cause of their mortality. In autumn, predators take on average over 60% of total numbers of bank voles and mice. However, when compared to densities of rodents (Figure 16.2), predation appeared to have its strongest effect at low rodent numbers, and played only a negligible role during periods of high rodent densities. Therefore, in the deciduous and mixed woodlands of Białowieża, predators play an inferior role in governing the populations of rodents. The principal role in driving their fluctuations is taken over by food: green vegetation on the forest floor that strongly varies between spring-summer and autumn-winter seasons, and the seed crops of forest trees, which show even greater variation from year to year.

Interestingly, mast-dependent outbreak-and-crash cycles (in otherwise moderate seasonal fluctuations of rodents) have noticeable

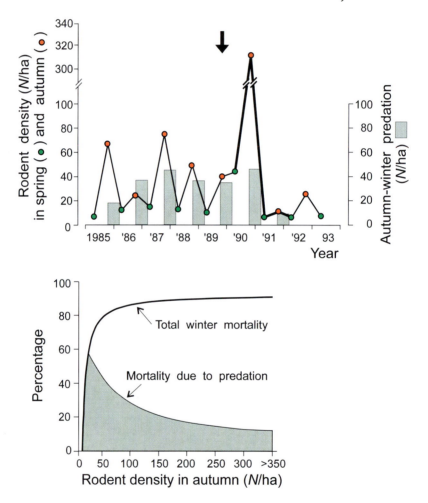

Figure 16.2. The role of predation in autumn and winter mortalities of forest rodents (bank voles and yellow-necked mice) in Białowieża Forest. Upper graph shows total autumn-winter predation by tawny owls, weasels, and pine martens in relation to rodent densities. Arrow denotes a heavy crop of tree seeds. Lower graphs shows the percent winter mortality of rodents in relation to their autumn densities and the role of predation (combined effect of the three predators) in total winter mortality. (Reprinted from: *Acta Theriologica* 41: 1–34, 1996; modified.)

impacts on the population dynamics of forest birds. First, these two groups of small vertebrates are linked through common predators. In years of a rodent crash, predators such as tawny owls, pine martens, common buzzards, and pygmy owls exert heavier tolls than usual on these birds, including their eggs and hatchlings. Medium-sized and large birds, especially those nesting on the ground, in shrubs, and in large cavities suffer the greatest losses from predators in such years (Figure 16.3). Not only has their breeding success been markedly lower in rodent crash years, but the number of adult birds also declined markedly during crash and post-crash years. Declines by over one-fourth of usual densities were recorded in hazel hens, woodcocks, robins, dunnocks, great spotted woodpeckers, and three-toed woodpeckers. Interestingly, birds nesting in small cavities

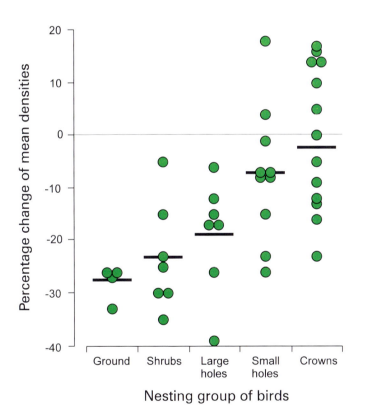

Figure 16.3. Percentage change of mean densities of birds in Białowieża National Park in years of low densities of forest rodents (crash and post--crash years – heavy pressure of predators on birds) as compared with years of moderate and high densities of rodents (average pressure of predators on birds) in relation to the height and type of nest location. Each point denotes one bird species. Bars are mean values in each group. (Reprinted from: *Predation in vertebrate communities.* Springer Verlag, Berlin, 1998.)

and high in tree canopies were significantly less, if at all, affected by increased predation (Figure 16.3).

Secondly, rodents themselves are effective predators on the tiny, delicate eggs of small-sized bird species. When densities of rodents are high, they are deadly enemies to wrens, wood warblers, and collared flycatchers. The breeding success of these birds is lowest (12–34%) in years of rodent outbreaks. One of these species, the wood warbler (a tropical migrant), has evolved the ability to assess rodent densities in forests to determine whether or not to settle in a location and breed. Over 20-years of data from Białowieża National Park show that densities of wood warbler breeding pairs are negatively correlated with those of rodents. How are these little birds able to assess the abundance of rodents? Possibly, as was found for some species of raptors, wood warblers are capable of seeing urine marks left by rodents in ultraviolet light.

A phenomenon at the European scale

Oaks (the common or English oak and the sessile oak) are keystone species of European lowland deciduous and mixed forests, which stretch from the Ural Mountains to the Atlantic coast. Interestingly, because summer temperatures stimulate the heaviest seed crops of oaks in years of flower-bud formation, the largest crops (recorded from 1958–1959, 1967–1968, 1977–1978, and 1983) occurred in synchrony from Moscow to southern England (Figure 16.4). Equally synchronous were the outbreaks of forest rodents caused by these seed crops.

In addition to geographic synchrony of the largest acorn crops, there is a strong east-west gradient in increasing fructification of oaks. Oak woods near Moscow produce only small or non-existent crops from one big mast till the next, whereas oak woods in Denmark and England usually yield one or two fair-sized crops in the same time span. As a consequence, outbreak densities of bank voles and mice occur more often in western than in eastern Europe.

From west to east, other important tree species often coexisting with oaks are beech, hornbeams, maples (Norway maples), sycamores, large-leaved limes, and small-leaved limes. Beech and oak-beech forests in the west, oak-lime-hornbeam forests in central Europe, and pine-lime-oak forests in the European part of Russia form a climatically determined gradient of forest types in lowland Europe. Wherever they form a significant part of tree stands, all these

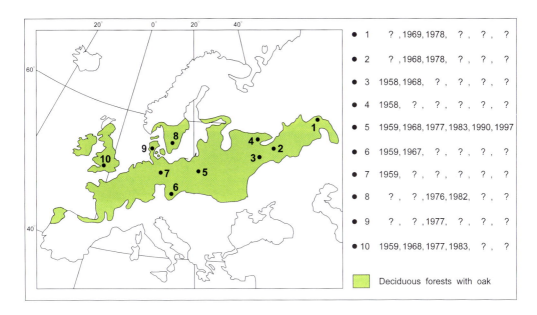

Figure 16.4. Spatial synchronization of the heaviest oak seed crops recorded in the geographic range of European deciduous forests with oaks. Points and numbers (1–10) indicate locations where studies on seed crop and/or rodent dynamics were conducted. Question marks indicate that no data were available. (Reprinted from: *Polish Journal of Ecology* 48, Suppl.: 163–177, 2000.)

deciduous species can drive mast-dependent fluctuations in population densities of forest rodents. In beech, abundant seed crops occur at 2- to 10-year intervals (on average 4 years), and they seldom coincide with those of oak. No crops usually occur after mast years. Outbreaks of forest rodents caused by heavy seed crops of beech were reported from the Ukraine, southern Poland, Denmark, and England.

It must be emphasized that mast-dependent dynamics of forest rodents, and the whole chain of trophic events they trigger in forest ecosystems, can only occur in mature deciduous and mixed forests. In most of Europe, however, natural old-growth forests have been exploited for centuries and transformed into fast-growing pine or spruce monocultures. With the decline of pristine deciduous woodlands in Europe, the ecological processes that involve seeds, rodents, and their predators may only be observed in scattered locations, such as Białowieża Primeval Forest.

Suggested readings

Hansson L., Jędrzejewska B. and Jędrzejewski W. 2000. Regional differences in dynamics of bank vole populations in Europe. [In: Bank vole biology: Recent advances in the population biology of a model species. G. Bujalska and L. Hansson, eds]. Polish Journal of Ecology 48, Suppl.: 163–177.

Jędrzejewska B. and Jędrzejewski W. 1998. Predation in vertebrate communities. The Białowieża Primeval Forest as a case study. Springer Verlag, Berlin – New York: 1–450.

Jędrzejewski W., Jędrzejewska B., Szymura A. and Zub K. 1996. Tawny owl (*Strix aluco*) predation in a pristine deciduous forest (Białowieża National Park, Poland). Journal of Animal Ecology 65: 105–120.

Pucek Z., Jędrzejewski W., Jędrzejewska B. and Pucek M. 1993. Rodent population dynamics in a primeval deciduous forest (Białowieża National Park) in relation to weather, seed crop, and predation. Acta Theriologica 38: 199–232.

Wesołowski T. and Tomiałojć L. 1997. Breeding bird dynamics in a primaeval temperate forest: long-term trends in Białowieża National Park (Poland). Ecography 20: 432–453.

17

Voles in river valleys

Joanna Gliwicz and Elżbieta Jancewicz

Voles of the genus Microtus are inhabitants of open grassy areas. In Białowieża Forest they live predominantly in river valleys, a network of relatively narrow strips of marshlands framed by vast forests. Of the three vole species that can be encountered in these areas, the root vole is the most common, though other rodent species are also present. Due to its occasionally very high biomass, and high-amplitude fluctuations in numbers from one year to another, the root vole forms the most important, though destabilising, component of this community.

Fluctuations in vole abundance

The dynamics of voles in the marshy habitats of the Narewka river valley in Białowieża Forest, as studied in 1986–2003, showed a multiannual pattern of a 3-year cycle in vole density (Figure 17.1A). In 1997–2003, a more detailed study of the root vole population was conducted at Reski Marsh in the Narewka river valley. It revealed less evidence of regular variations, however it supported the existence of the high multiannual fluctuations (Figure 17.1B). Root vole density in the annual peaks (in summer or in autumn) of different years ranged 45-fold, from 2 to nearly 90 individuals per hectare. At the same time, seasonal variations between the lowest density in the spring and the highest in summer or autumn, were lower, from 5 to 26 fold. Thus, to recognize the factors driving vole density, we should focus on an explanation of multiannual patterns.

What are the consequences of these multiannual fluctuations for the whole community? The average biomass of the root vole was

960 grams per hectare during the vegetation season (May–September) and 710 gram per hectare during winter (October–April). The root vole was the primary component of the rodent community, making up 70% of the whole biomass. Thus, the entire biomass of small rodents was, on average, 1325 grams per hectare in summer and 1020 grams per hectare in winter. This was the "offer" of the meadow community to the mammalian and avian predators dependent on rodents for food. In Białowieża Forest, there are at least 4 mammal and 6 raptor species in whose diets rodents constitute an important component in the summer period. There are 5 mammalian and 5 avian species for whom they are crucial in winter. The predators hunt in the forest and in the meadows, depending on the relative density of rodents. However, in both habitats rodent densities and biomass vary greatly from year to year (see also Chapter 16).

In the meadows, the root vole fluctuations drive the overall changes in rodent biomass available to predators. This is due to two factors. Firstly, the root vole is the largest rodent of the meadow community, therefore changes in their numbers have a high impact on the rodent biomass. Secondly, they are the preferred prey species

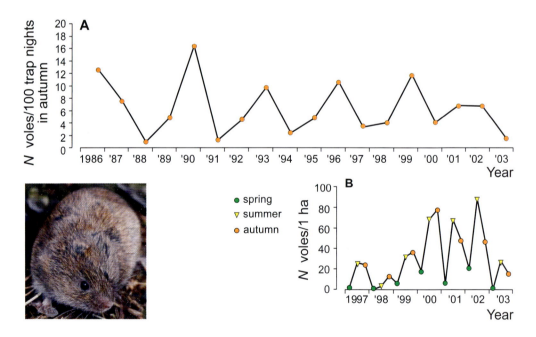

Figure 17.1. Multiannual changes in the abundance of the root vole in the Narewka river valley, Białowieża Forest: (A) based on trapping in autumn at seven meadow sites; (B) results of live-trapping and individual marking on a 1-hectare plot in Reski Marsh, the Narewka river valley. Photo by Zbigniew Borowski.

due to their size, palatability, and relatively slow movements. However, they are not a very dependable resource. In 1998, the year of their lowest density, their average biomass in summer was only 90 g per hectare (and those of the whole meadow rodent community 350 g per hectare). In 2000, when root voles were most abundant, their biomass in the summer was 20 times higher (1,725 g per hectare), and it made up 96% of all rodent biomass.

Such changes in the food availability are especially disruptive for specialist predators strictly dependent on rodents, such as the weasel. In this respect however, the forest-meadow system of the Białowieża Forest offers the predators unusually favourable conditions in the form of two independently fluctuating, non-synchronised rodent communities, living in two adjacent habitats, with a very long border line. This is probably the reason for the very high weasel densities here (see Chapter 14).

Another aspect of the fluctuations in root vole density, is their impact on vegetation in the marshy habitats. The root vole is a folivorous species, feeding mostly on sedges. During the season of vegetation it consumes their stems, blades and young sprouts, and in winter – the underground roots and partly on dead biomass. These voles also depend on sedge tussocks for their nest and corridor constructions, and when digging and biting out the plant tissue at the base of tussocks, they may additionally damage the vegetation. A rough estimation of yearly consumption, based on the vole's known biomass, energy requirements and food assimilation rates, leads to the following results. During the seven years of the study in Reski Marsh, the average annual consumption by root voles was equivalent of about 50 kg of dry mass of green vegetation per hectare. These figures differed 7-fold between the lowest and the highest year of vole abundance, being 12 and 80 kg, respectively. However, even in the year with the highest consumption, this mass only corresponds to about 1.2–1.5% of the total annual production of temperate zone grasslands, assumed here to be 6,000–7,000 kg dry mass per hectare. Yet it is possible that not only the value of plant consumption, but more importantly a sudden increase, coupled with the mechanical damage at high vole densities, will affect feeding conditions for other sedge meadow inhabitants. This would explain, at least partly, some of the observed changes in the numbers and diversity of other rodents in the study area, which show negative correlation with vole density. This could also, at least theoretically, limit food availability for subsequent generations of the root voles, and cause their cyclic dynamics.

Let us assume that the observed high multiannual fluctuation in the root vole numbers, despite their irregular nature basically follow a 3-year cycle occasionally disrupted by some external factor. This pattern of population dynamics in rodents has been much studied, and many factors that can potentially drive it, by producing a sufficient time lag in the density response of a rodent population, have been indicated. The factors most frequently tested by contemporary rodent scientists, are the effects of specialist predators, food, parasites and diseases. The first of the above hypotheses, indicating a specialist predator, and more precisely the weasel as the reason for vole cycles is the most popular. Root vole – weasel interactions were studied in detail at the Reski site, and were found to be an unlikely factor responsible for vole dynamics in the area (see Chapter 14). The number of weasels present in the meadow seems to depend on the relative abundance of rodents in the meadow and forest. There was no time lag observed in the numerical response of weasels to fluctuations in vole density, hence weasels act as a factor disrupting regularity of the vole cycles rather than driving it. As for the effect of food, considering how very small a fraction of plant production (or biomass) is required by voles to cover their energy demands, this hypothesis is not very promising. Finally, nothing is known at the moment about the parasite infestation of rodents inhabiting the Białowieża Forest. In summary, we do not know what causes multiannual fluctuations in the vole populations, only what may influence their irregularity.

Where root voles prefer to live

The root vole is an interesting species due to its preference for humid, seasonally-flooded grassy habitats. Such habitats in Europe are less common than they were in the past, due to profound changes in water level, river regulation and farming practices. Loss of these habitats is responsible for a decrease in the biodiversity of marshland species across Europe. The root vole has become less common too; its range contracting, its local populations more isolated and, in case of some subspecies (*Microtus oeconomus mehelyi* in Hungary or *M. o. arenicola* in the Netherlands), even threatened. In our study in Reski Marsh we focused on the analysis of the preferences shown by the root vole towards some characteristic features of the marshland area. The area was moderately heterogeneous in respect to ground humidity, presence of willow shrubs, patches of forbs (especially the meadowsweet) locally interspaced with sedges and grasses, and to vegetation cover thickness at ground level. All root voles preferred more humid and open places, far from shrubs. Additionally, females avoided sites with a dense cover of perennial forbs. Sedge and grass cover was evidently sufficient throughout the study plot, because no preferences in this respect were observed.

Another interesting question is whether adult males and females show any difference in their habitat preference. We expected that females, bearing almost all the reproduction costs, would be more selective in respect to local conditions, which may secure better survival for them and their offspring, and result in high reproductive success. Furthermore, in the years of low density, the individuals should choose the most preferred sites for locating their home ranges, but with increasing density, some of them would be forced to less preferred sites.

Our results fully supported this hypothesis and assumption (Figure 17.2). Females, when free to choose the best places, showed

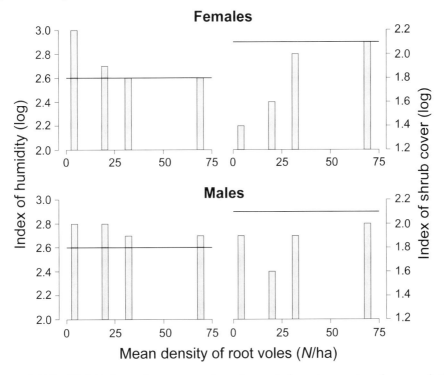

Figure 17.2. Habitat preferences of male and female root voles, and their changes with increasing population density. Bars show average ground humidity (left) and shrub cover (right) in the localities inhabited by voles in years of different densities. Average humidity and shrub cover for the whole meadow plot are indicated by lines. For females, the humidity of inhabited sites correlates negatively, and the shrub cover positively with increasing density, indicating limited choice of good sites at higher densities.

preference for the most humid sites with no shrubs in the vicinity, and their preference was more marked than that of males. The gradual increase in female acceptance of less optimal sites with increasing population density well illustrates the deterioration of breeding conditions, and may be considered as a potential factor of the density regulation process. Males did not show any significant changes in this respect.

What can be inferred from the revealed microhabitat preferences of the root voles, particularly apparent in the female root voles? We propose that the avoidance of shrubs means avoidance of potential shelters for mammalian predators, which can be more easily spotted in the open. The favouring of wetter sites correlates with the preference for larger sedge tussocks (growing in more humid spots) that offer better conditions for nest location and/or more fresh green sprouts for food.

Home ranges and spatial behaviour

In order to learn more about the spatial behavior of male and female root voles we combined live-trapping and radio-tracking techniques. Voles represent an interesting study object to behavioural ecologists because even closely related species differ in their spatial behavior. The root vole is among those vole species in which breeding females show a spatial intolerance of other breeding females, that is, they are intrasexually territorial. Male home ranges however overlap with each other, as well as with the territories of several females. Such a space use pattern is typical in promiscuous species, with the male mating all receptive females present within its home range, and the estrous female copulating with many males visiting her territory.

When analysing pooled results of our study in Reski Marsh and those of other studies conducted in two other localities in Poland (Masurian Lake District and Biebrza River Valley) and one in Norway, we found that under low and medium densities, home range size in males was about 750–800 m^2, and in females only about 300 m^2. But in the latter case, the territory was used exclusively by one owner. The size of observed female territories (202–377 m^2 in different studied localities) negatively correlated with the richness of local habitats. In higher densities, males decreased their home ranges to about 500–550 m^2, whereas the females' territories did not change in size. Instead, they became more tolerant towards other breeding females and home ranges were no longer used exclusively by a single female. The resulting spatial clumping of reproductive females at high density allowed the males to decrease their home range size without diminishing their chances for successful matings.

Additionally, when radio-tracking some adult males and females continuously for 24 hours in July, we gained a new insight into the exploratory behavior of voles moving inside their home ranges (Figure 17.3). Males did not only move over a larger area and cover longer distances (10 m on average) in each running episode, but they also explored the interior of a home range more uniformly, and visited its boundaries more often than the females. A breeding female was typically nursing or pregnant at the time of radio-tracking. She was most often located in the vicinity of a burrow, from which she made short excursions, usually to her preferred feeding spots, and then quickly returned to the burrow. The observed behaviour makes it clear why breeding females tend to maintain exclusive territories, and why they are so selective when choosing a place to live. They cannot afford to leave their offspring alone for a long time and, due to their high-energy demands (especially during

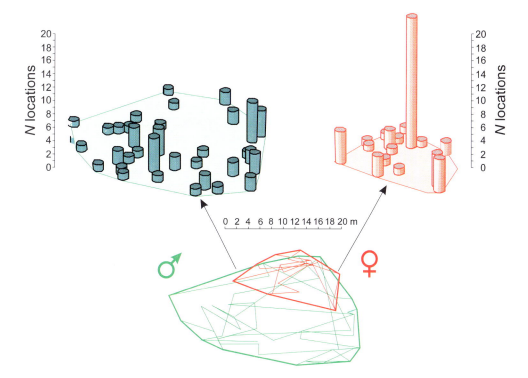

Figure 17.3. Exploration of the home range by root voles, as registered by 24-hour radio-tracking. The bars (upper graphs) indicate the frequency of visits to different sections of the home range by a male and a female. The lines (lower graph) connect the subsequent locations of the same pair of voles holding overlapping home ranges.

lactation), they need constant access to nourishing food resources, close to their nest burrows, without competition from neighbouring voles.

Other inhabitants of river valleys

The root vole, although by far a dominant species in the rodent community of marshy meadows of Białowieża, is regularly accompanied there by other species. In Reski Marsh, the following species are present: field vole, bank vole, striped field mouse, yellow-necked mouse, harvest mouse, and birch mouse. Four species of this assembly are significantly smaller in size than the dominant vole, and 5 of them are more agile. In this habitat, the prevalent success of the root vole results from its efficient exploitation of the available resources. Therefore, in years with high root vole densities, other species may experience shortages of vital resources. In years of low root vole density, populations of other rodent rapidly increase, and the overall rodent species diversity significantly increases (Figure 17.4).

The patterns of biodiversity change in the studied rodent community provides an interesting illustration of a concept of Robert Paine, who stated that "*local species diversity is directly related to the efficiency with which predator prevents the monopolization of the major environmental requisites by one species*". Paine tested his idea

Photo 17.1. Vole habitats in river valleys of the Białowieża Primeval Forest. Photo by Jan Walencik.

in experimental studies of intertidal marine communities, and later his concept received support from several empirical and theoretical research projects (none of them, however, dealt with mammal communities under natural conditions). Based on findings of these previous studies, the following conditions, favourable for diversity stimulating effects of predation, can be determined: strong competition among prey species, obvious dominance of one species, high susceptibility of the dominant species to predation, high intensity of predation, and spatial heterogeneity.

All these conditions are fulfilled in the ecological system studied in Białowieża. Let us briefly discuss them here. Among the resources for which the seven rodent inhabitants of the marshy meadows can compete (exploitation competition), food is not the obvious one. First of all, because the trophic niches of these rodents vary considerably. Seeds prevail in diets of all murid species, and the birch mouse feeds on seeds and invertebrates. Secondly, the green biomass of plants is produced in this humid grassland in great surplus in relation to rodent needs. However, space, and especially the microhabitats preferred by the root vole, may be in shortage in the years of its high numbers and may limit the numbers of less efficient competitors. The competition for space may be additionally reinforced by the

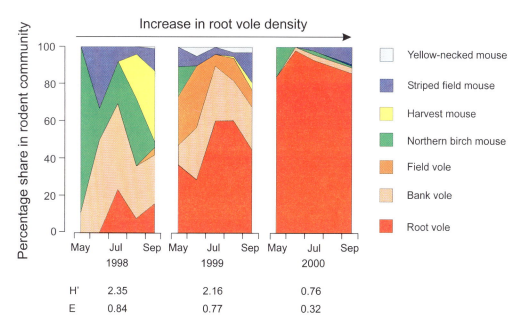

Figure 17.4. Shares of various species in a small rodent community in riverside marshes in years with low (1998), medium (1999) and high (2000) density of the root vole. Values of Shannon-Wiener index of diversity (H') and Equitability index (E) are given for each year.

interference competition between the root vole and other rodents, and in particular by the apparent competition. The high density of root voles probably attracts all kinds of predators, and makes the vole habitat unattractive or simply uninhabitable to other rodent species.

The obvious numerical dominance of the root vole in this assembly is corroborated by its average 70% share in the rodent community biomass on the meadow, as well as by the fact that diversity values (Shannon-Wiener index) of all rodents correlate negatively with root vole densities.

Rodents are generally an attractive prey to all types of predators, with large species such as the root vole being most attractive, because they offer the best energetic return for the predator's unit effort. Our direct observations in Reski Marsh proved that the root vole was the species most often attacked by weasels (see Chapter 14). In general, predator pressure in the Białowieża river valleys is very high due to the rich predator community and their numerous populations; and particularly due to very high weasel numbers that appear in some years in the marshy habitats. In such years they decimate the root vole population, and release space and other environmental requisites to other rodents, which are less attractive as prey species.

The spatial heterogeneity of the Białowieża Forest is important here in two aspects. Firstly, it offers alternative habitats to rodents excluded from the meadows during times of high vole densities, and hence prevents their extinction from the local system. Secondly, it provides alternative prey for weasels and maintains a diverse and abundant assembly of generalist predators. Due to these unique features of the study area and its surroundings, we could observe ecological mechanisms, which maintain biodiversity, at work.

Suggested readings

Gliwicz J. 1997. Space use in the root vole: basic patterns and variability. Ecography 20: 383–389.

Gliwicz J. 1996. Life history of voles: growth and maturation of seasonal cohorts of the root vole. Miscellanea Zoologica 19: 1–12.

Ostfeld R. S. 1985. Limiting resources and territoriality in microtine rodents. American Naturalist 126: 1–15.

Paine R. T. 1966. Food web complexity and species diversity. American Naturalist 100: 56–75.

18

Natural economy of mammalian energy budgets

Marek Konarzewski

All animals are what they eat. Energy contained in food is an essential fuel for all their needs. However, food is not freely available in the environment, and under most circumstances it is a rare commodity. Thus, all living things are forced to carefully manage their energy budgets. A closer look at mammalian energetics reveals a fascinating realm of mechanisms geared to the most efficient utilization of every consumed calorie.

Mammals – energetically expensive creatures

Undoubtedly, mammals are a good example of evolutionary success. They dwell in just about every habitat, from the Arctic to the tropics, and from dry deserts to open oceans. The key feature behind their evolutionary success is endothermy – the ability to maintain and strictly regulate body temperature, independent of ambient temperature. However, endothermy is energetically costly. On average, the cost of endothermy pushes the rate of energy consumption of mammals an order of magnitude higher than that of reptiles. How did mammalian endothermy evolve, and what are the essential pre- -requisites for their success?

Currently, two scenarios have been put forth to explain the evolution of endothermy. The first, proposed by Albert Benett and John Ruben in 1979, is known as the aerobic capacity model (Figure

18.1, left). According to this model, the driving force behind the evolution of endothermy was the selection for speed and stamina in mammalian predecessors. High speed and stamina required an increase in the aerobic capacity of muscles involved in locomotion. On the physiological level, this manifested itself as an increased peak (or summit) metabolic rate (PMR). However, the capacity to achieve this bore a cost: muscles capable of high metabolic rates had to incorporate more mitochondria, whose biochemical properties allowed them to generate maximum power in a short time. This machinery, even when running idle, consumes a lot of energy, which is dissipated in the form of heat. According to the aerobic capacity model, this high rate of compulsory heat production gave rise to the maintenance of stable body temperatures, independent of ambient temperatures.

A simple illustration of this mechanism is the comparison of two cars, say a small Fiat and a powerful Porsche, running idle in front of a red traffic light. The small engine of the Fiat consumes little fuel,

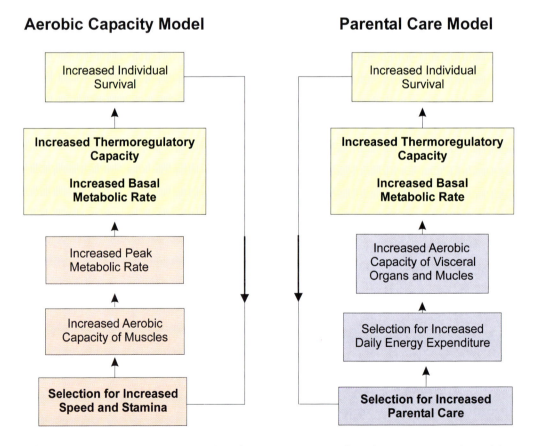

Figure 18.1. Box-chart models of the evolution of endothermy predicted by the aerobic capacity model (left) and the parental care model (right).

whereas the big engine of the Porsche consumes considerable amount of fuel. However, when the light turns green, it is the Porsche that starts and goes really fast. This is exactly what the Porsches were built for, with the expense of wasteful fuel consumption, even at the lowest revolution rate. Mammals and birds are such "sport cars" among living organisms. Their high aerobic capacity is inexorably linked with the generation of extra heat, and the energetic costs of maintaining their power-generating metabolic machinery. This, in turn, manifests itself as a high basal metabolic rate (BMR, the biological equivalent of a car running idle). The aerobic capacity model therefore predicts that a high BMR is a by-product of selection for increased speed and stamina, and that the two evolved in concert, increasing individual survival (Figure 18.1, left).

There are, however, some important problems inherent with the evolutionary scenario proposed by the aerobic capacity model; one being that at least half the metabolic costs incorporated in the BMR are generated by metabolically expensive internal organs, such as the intestines, kidneys, liver, and heart. Among them, only the heart's metabolic capacity is directly related to the generation of metabolic power immediately required to achieve high speed and stamina. The other organs are involved in processes related to the maintenance of high energy assimilation rates and the elimination of metabolic waste products. This is clearly incompatible with selection for short metabolic bursts, as suggested by the aerobic capacity model, and rather points to the selection for high levels of metabolic expenditures maintained over longer periods of time (e.g. weeks or even months). In the long run, maintaining high daily energy expenditure (DEE) levels would be impossible without a sizable increase of the visceral organs associated with energy assimilation, which in turn significantly contributes to an increased BMR. This suggests the evolution of high BMR, and consequently endothermy, was largely driven by selection favoring a high, sustainable locomotor activity fueled by an aerobic metabolism. Because the sustained locomotor activity most immediately associated with Darwinian fitness is parental care, the need to feed and guard offspring (rather than metabolic bursts incurred by short episodes of chasing prey or escaping predators), may have been the driving force behind the evolution of endothermy (Figure 18.1, right).

Unfortunately, neither behaviour nor physiological traits preserve well in paleontological records. How can one meaningfully test the evolutionary scenarios depicted in Figure 18.1? The most straightforward way would be to test alternative predictions of the two models in extant animals (Figure 18.2). A close, positive relationship between Peak Metabolic Rate and Basal Metabolic Rate would point to the validity of the aerobic capacity model. Alternatively, a tight relationship between Daily Energy Expenditure and BMR would favour the parental care model.

In the last few decades, both models have been repeatedly tested by comparative methods involving interspecies comparisons. So far, results have been largely equivocal: a weak, positive association between BMR and DEE seems to exist in mammals, but not in birds. In neither of these taxa is there a close link between BMR and PMR. The matter undoubtedly awaits more decisive tests. A new and promising approach takes advantage of quantitative genetics.

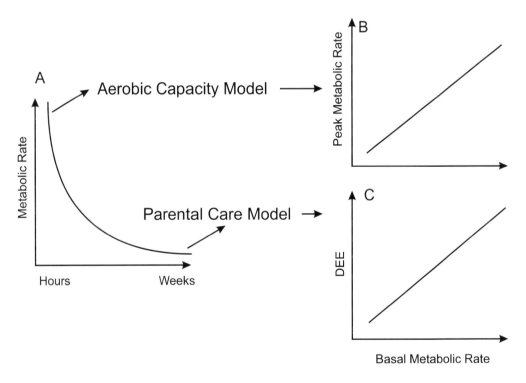

Figure 18.2. Consequences of the relationship between the metabolic rate and its duration (A); for the predictions stemming from the aerobic capacity model (B); and parental care model (C). Natural selection for short, metabolic bursts should result in a positive link between Peak Metabolic Rate and Basal Metabolic Rate, predicted by the aerobic capacity model. Conversely, the selection for intense parental care should result in maximizing the sustained metabolic rate (SusMR), usually estimated as Daily Energy Expenditures (DEE) and therefore, positively associated with SusMR and BMR.

Indeed, in terms of quantitative genetics both models predict not only a strong, phenotypic association between BMR and DEE (or BMR and PMR), but more importantly a genetic correlation between them. That is, individuals carrying genes for high PMR should inexorably carry the genes for high BMR, if the aerobic capacity model holds true. Conversely, a genetic correlation between BMR and DEE should point to the validity of the parental care model. One way to test this would be to mimic the action of natural selection by artificially selecting for DEE or PMR and following the changes in BMR. Currently, there are at least three independent attempts worldwide to artificially select rodent species: laboratory mice (Photo 18.1) and bank voles, for specific metabolic traits. Hopefully, these experiments will yield decisive solutions to the puzzle surrounding the evolution of endothermy.

Photo 18.1. Laboratory mouse in a metabolic chamber. Photo by Andrzej Gębczyński.

Natural economy of energy budgets

Managing a home budget can be a tricky task. The same applies to the energy management of every individual. In this case natural selection would be the manager. Exploring the solutions to manage the energetic needs of individual organisms is a task of both physiology and ecology. From an ecological point of view, the obvious constraint imposed on any wild animal's energy budget is the availability of energy in the environment (Figure 18.3). However, convincing evidence suggests that during important stages of their life cycles, animals may not be limited by the amount of available energy in the environment. For example, in many food supplementation experiments, mammals and birds did not respond to extra food by increases in reproductive output. Furthermore, when corrected for body mass, the maximum energy assimilation rate of animals subjected to extreme metabolic demands, such as cold-stressed weasels, fast growing broiler chickens and dedicated human athletes, was surprisingly similar. This suggests that energy expenditures could be limited by some internal, physiological constraints, rather than an external (environmental) supply of energy. Analysis of such

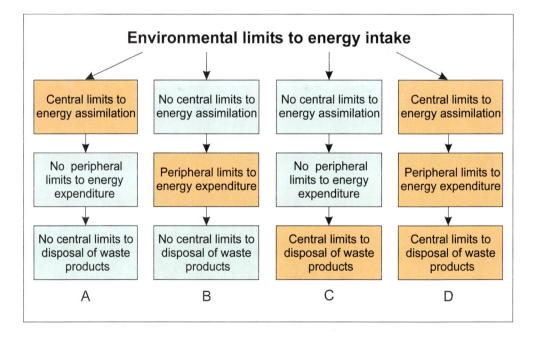

Figure 18.3. Box-chart models of the effects of environmental and physiological constraints on energy utilization. Hypothetical bottlenecks within the systems are depicted by red colour.

constraints has revealed that "design limitations" have been imposed on mammalian metabolic machinery.

The first possible constraint may be on the rate at which food is broken down and digested. In general, mammals consume two types of food: (1) energetically dense and easily digestible foods, such as flesh of other animals, nutritious seeds and delicate parts of plants; or (2) fiber-rich, difficult to digest plant food. Energy-rich foods are scarce and difficult to collect, but once obtained, they do not require much extra time and energy to be digested. Consequently, the digestive tract of carnivores, for example, has a simple structure and constitutes a small proportion of their body mass. Most mammalian herbivores forage on readily available, but almost indigestible plant foods, so they need large guts to allow for fermentation and decomposition. Therefore, herbivores are more prone to those constraints associated with digestion.

There is, however, yet another important concept behind possible energy intake limits imposed by digestive processes. Because the rate of assimilation/digestion constitutes the first step in energy flow through an organism, any constraints imposed on it limits the energy available down-stream in the metabolic cascade (Figure 18.3, pathway A). In this sense, the rate of digestion is the main limiting factor with respect to the remaining steps of energy use and processing. However, it is also possible that under some conditions, it is not the rate of assimilation that limits energy flow (and ultimately an animal's metabolic performance), but rather some constraints on the rate of energy use in one of the peripheral body components, which is fueled by already assimilated energy (Figure 18.3, pathway B). For example, the maximum rate of an animal's long-term locomotor activity may be constrained by the capacity of its muscles to withstand physical stress of a workload, rather than by the ability of its digestive tract to extract enough energy and nutrients to meet the energetic demands of muscular work. Another limiting factor, this time imposing the constraint up-stream in the metabolic cascade, limits the rate at which waste products (generated by all elements of the cascade) are eliminated (Figure 18.3, pathway C). Thus, from the "design" point of view, physiological constraints on energy management may reside in the physiological processes underlying either "supply/sanitation" organ systems (digestive tract and kidneys) or "demand" systems (muscles, mammary glands).

Finally, the metabolic pathway's subsequent steps may have adjusted to one another, so none of them constitutes a bottleneck in the system (Figure 18.3, pathway D). It is important to note, that the existence of any bottleneck in a physiological system implies that the cascade's non-limiting steps are not being used to their utmost capacity. Thus, from an economic point of view, the optimal design is that characterized by the lack of any bottleneck, or symmorphic.

How can one detect, under particular environmental conditions which system(s) act as a constraint, or whether their components are indeed symmorphic? One way of tackling this problem is to compare maximum energy assimilation rates under various conditions by imposing metabolic stress on different combinations of peripheral organs. A uniform maximum energy assimilation rate, and its close match with energetic demands of peripheral systems (in animals subject to different metabolic stressors) would indicate that constraints on energy management reside in central supply/sanitation systems. This has been tested by manipulating the energy intake of laboratory mice, whose energy budgets were pushed to their physiological limits by long-term cold exposure, intense lactation or a combination of the two. Mice burdened with lactation were able to increase their energy assimilation rate far more than those subjected to cold-stress. Furthermore, the energy assimilation rate of mice forced to lactate in the cold was still higher. These results indicate that the constraints on energy budgets reside in peripheral systems, as the digestive capacity of the gut was flexible enough to meet the energetic needs of mice even under extremely demanding conditions.

To some extent, such functional flexibility is typical for most physiological processes. It stems from a so-called reserve capacity built into almost all biological structures, which allow animals to tide over unexpected metabolic challenges. Clearly, however, the notion of a reserve capacity (often referred to as a safety margin, and defined as the ratio of the maximum load to the average load) is difficult to reconcile with the postulated and purely symmorphic character of the physiological design. This is because symmorphic design assumes a rigid and static match of the capacities of subsequent elements of the physiological cascade. In contrast, the notion of reserve capacity rises the question of the significance of environmental unpredictability, and evolutionary incorporation of its effects into the physiological design. Thus, as eminent American biologist Jared Diamond put it, the major question is: "How much of the physiological capacity is enough, but not too much".

All mammals, big and small

Mammals are characterized by having the greatest body size variation among all animals. The smallest species, American pygmy shrew, can sit comfortably in a teaspoon, whereas the largest, the blue whale, weighs over 30 tons. From an evolutionary point of view, the optimal size is one that maximizes fitness, that is, lifetime reproductive success. The very existence of a shrew and a whale clearly shows that there is no single optimum for mammalian body size.

Why, then, are mammalian body sizes so diversified? There are two main factors governing optimal size: (1) production rate, that is, the rate at which energy can be converted into new tissues, contributing to an increase in body size, and (2) mortality.

In the simplest form, the production rate $P(w)$ can be described by the equation:

$$P(w) = A(w) - R(w),$$

where $A(w)$ is resource acquisition rate, $R(w)$ is metabolic rate and w is body size. For most organisms, both $A(w)$ and $R(w)$ can be approximated by the following power functions:

$$A(w) = aw^b \text{ and } R(w) = cw^d,$$

where b and d are so called allometric exponents, whose values typically fall between $2/3$ and 1. Further, interesting insights into the properties of $P(w)$, $A(w)$ and $R(w)$ can be gained when they are plotted on a double logarithmic scale. The use of a logarithmic, rather than an arithmetic scale allows one to accommodate in one graph the range of body sizes of a mouse and an elephant. Furthermore, log-transformation allows to graphically present rather unfriendly power functions as straight lines with slopes equal to b and d for $A(w)$ and $R(w)$, respectively. Such a plot reveals that the difference between $A(w)$ and $R(w)$ is relatively greater for smaller, rather than larger animals (Figure 18.4 A). Furthermore, there exists the body size for which $A(w) = R(w)$, and therefore growing beyond such a body size is impossible.

Growing to a certain size takes time. All things being equal, the probability of survival to a certain age decreases exponentially with time, and for this very reason, when the mortality rate is high, it does not pay to grow to a large body size. It is obvious, therefore, that the mortality rate determines whether to allocate production to further growth or shunt it to reproduction: under heavy mortality an investment in growth is likely to be lost. However, the story is not all that simple. Under realistic ecological conditions, both production rate and mortality, often depend on body size. There are many potential predators preying on small rodents, but very few would dare to attack a European bison. For this reason, it sometimes pays to grow to a gigantic body size, and thus escape a high mortality rate. Such a strategy, however, bears an important cost: a low production rate due to the convergence of $A(w)$ and $R(w)$ at larger body sizes (Figure 18.4A). This translates to a very low reproduction rate, which is sufficient to maintain a stable population size under constant environmental conditions. However, any catastrophic environmental changes, such as an abrupt climatic change or a new predator, could bring giants on the brink of extinction. This was probably the reason for the sudden demise (on a geological time scale) of the representatives of so-called megafauna, for example, giant ground sloths and mammoths, which roamed Eurasia and North America 15 thousand years ago. Their extinction, at the end of the Ice Age, can be likely attributed to global warming and the invasion of the most effective of all predators, *Homo sapiens*.

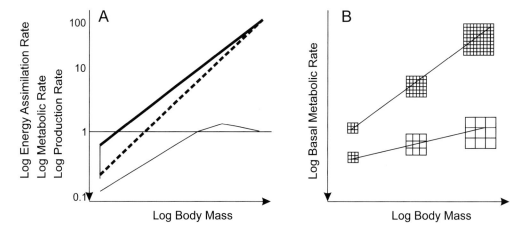

Figure 18.4. (A) The rate of production of an organism (thin, solid line) is the difference between the rate of energy assimilation rate (thick solid line) and the metabolic (respiration) rate (dotted line). Note that all relationships are depicted on a logarithmic scale. (B) The relationship between body size and metabolic rate in two hypothetical, evolutionary lineages originating from species of similar body size. The upper line represents allometry of metabolic rate in three exemplary species of the lineage, in which an increase in body size has been realized entirely through an increase in the numbers of equally-sized cells. The lower line represents allometry in the representatives of the lineage, in which an increase in body mass was realized by an increase in cell size. (Reprinted from: *Proceedings of the National Academy of Sciences*, USA 100: 14080–14085, 2003; modified.)

Figure 18.4A shows that the production rate depends on the differences in the slopes and elevations of the lines representing $A(w)$ and $R(w)$. The slope of $R(w)$ has attracted particular attention, because it appears to be mirrored in the slopes relating body size with many key ecological and physiological traits, such as home range and longevity. Its value is lower than 1, and therefore, it increases less than proportionally with body size. For this reason, when expressed by body mass unit, the metabolic rate of larger mammals is lower than that of smaller ones. The search for an explanation of this puzzling phenomenon has continued for over the past hundred years. Currently, there are at least two hypotheses put forward to explain it. One suggests that the very nature of fractal-like supply systems (such as vertebrate circulatory and ventilatory systems) constitute a rate limiting step in the O_2 delivery cascade, and thus govern the scaling of the whole-body basal metabolic rate. The other hypothesis refers to the systematic differences of cell metabolism.

Consider the evolutionary process of body size increase in a lineage of closely related species (Figure 18.4B). This increase can be realized by either an increase in cell number or cell size. When an increase in body size is achieved by an increase in cell number, the whole body metabolism increases proportionally with body size, because it is built of more units of similar size. As a result, the relationship between metabolic rate and body size has a slope equal to 1. However, when an increase in size is realized through cell size increase, the surface of each cell, relative to its volume, decreases (this follows from simple Euclidean geometry: the volume of a sphere scales to the 3rd power, whereas its surface scales to the 2nd power). This has important metabolic consequences, because a substantial proportion of the metabolic rate reflects the energetic costs of maintaining ionic gradients across cell membranes. Thus, when an organism is built of larger cells, its metabolic intensity (i.e. metabolic rate per unit mass) is lower, as compared with a similar-sized organism but built of smaller cells. As a consequence, the relationship between metabolic rate and body size among organisms built of larger and larger cells has a slope equal to $2/3$, reflecting the change in cell surface to volume ratio (Figure 18.4B). In reality, the evolution of body size has been realized by both an increase in cell number and cell size, and therefore, the metabolic rate scales to $3/4$ (intermediate value between $2/3$ and 1).

In this quick tour through energetics I have focused on just a few areas of research. The nature of energy management studies make them incredible interfaces between such apparently distant fields as cell and molecular biology, genetics, evolutionary biology and ecology. The integrative character of energetic research will continue to incorporate different fields of modern biology into environmental sciences.

Suggested readings

Alexander R. M. 1998. Symmorphosis and safety factors. [In: Principles of animal design. The optimization and symmorphosis debate, E. R. Weibel, C. R. Taylor and L. Bolis, eds]. Cambridge University Press, Cambridge: 21–27.

Benett A. F. and Ruben J. A. 1979. Endothermy and activity in vertebrates. Science 206: 649–654.

Hammond K., Konarzewski M., Lerma R. and Diamond J. 1994. Metabolic ceilings under combination of peak energy demands. Physiological Zoology 67: 1479–1506.

Koteja P. 2000. Energy assimilation, parental care and the evolution of endothermy. Proceedings of the Royal Society of London B 267: 479–484.

Kozłowski J., Konarzewski M. and Gawełczyk A. 2003. Cell size as a link between non-coding DNA and metabolic rate scaling. Proceedings of the National Academy of Sciences, USA 100: 14080–14085.

West G. B., Brown J. H. and Enquist B. J. 1997. A general model for the origin of allometric scaling laws in biology. Nature 276: 122–126.

19

Competition and coexistence of shrews

Leszek Rychlik

Shrews are the smallest, but, due to their extremely high metabolic rate, the most voracious mammals. They are also very sensitive to biological and environmental factors. Therefore, shrews have to be more effective in foraging and resource extorting from competitors than most other mammals. Although some shrew species are difficult to distinguish by sight, they display some subtle and impressive differences in behaviour. These characteristics make them excellent models for a number of biological studies, including those on competition.

Small and voracious

Most shrews are very small animals with body masses of 5 to 15 g. The smallest species, the pygmy white-toothed shrew, weights 2 g and is the smallest mammal in the world. On the other hand, the metabolic rate of shrews is the highest among mammals. It is, for example, 5 times higher than in small rodents of comparable size (e.g. harvest mice). This results in the extremely voracious nature of shrews. They are active year round and many hours per day, mostly busy with foraging. They eat such large amounts (up to 350% of their body mass per day) and so frequently, they had to evolve a way to postpone the wearing of their teeth – this was achieved by incorporating some iron into the tooth tips (which results in their red coloration). Shrews are very sensitive to even subtle changes in food availability, climatic conditions, and density of intra- or interspecific competitors. Thus, to avoid death from starvation, they have to be more effective hunters than other predators.

Five species of shrews occur in Białowieża Forest. Among these, the masked shrew is extremely rare and confined only to a few habitats (see Chapter 3). More numerous are two terrestrial species (the pygmy shrew and common shrew) and two semi-aquatic ones (the Mediterranean water shrew and Eurasian water shrew). They co-exist in wet habitats such as sedge swamps, ash-alder forests, wet meadows and reeds in river valleys and along forest streams. They differ considerably in body size and basic metabolic rate. The pygmy shrew (Photo 19.1) is the smallest (3 g) but has the highest metabolic rate, whereas the Eurasian water shrew is the largest (14 g) with the lowest metabolic rate. Intermediate values were found for the common shrew (8 g) and Mediterranean water shrew (10 g). The latter species, exceptional among soricine shrews, is gregarious and intra-specifically tolerant. In contrast, the three other species are very aggressive, solitary and territorial.

Foraging strategies of shrews

Natural diets of both small and large shrew species include many types of tiny prey (<5 mm long: mites, spiders, daddy-long-legs, certain beetles and bugs), and even very small shrews take some large prey (>30 mm: earthworms, caterpillars, fly larvae, snails). However, shrews differ in body size, bite force and morphological adaptations. This must lead to interspecific differences in foraging behaviour and prey preferences. Laboratory experiments (including manipulations of distribution, quantity and size of prey, and infra--red video recording) were performed to reveal such differences among the four species of shrews co-existing in Białowieża Forest.

These experiments showed that shrews use two distinct strategies when searching for prey: a random searching pattern when foraging on land, and foraging in a one-dimensional habitat when foraging in water. In the first strategy, which is commonly used by terrestrial shrews foraging on the ground surface or in upper layers of litter and soil (e.g. the common shrew), prey is located in a random but thorough process of searching in a patch. In the second strategy, semi-aquatic shrews searching for aquatic prey take routes composed of long, straight travelling stretches along water banks with relatively lengthy stops for hunting in chosen patches. Eurasian water shrews were observed in the wild to dive repeatedly in the same spot of a stream after detecting clusters of prey under the surface. This strategy is an adaptation to exploit clustered food resources, whereas the random searching pattern is effective in searching for dispersed terrestrial prey.

These experiments also showed a fundamental relationship: the larger the shrew, the more prey it ate per capita. For example, Eurasian water shrews ate ca. 4.5 times more food than pygmy shrews and 1.5 times more than common shrews and Mediterranean water shrews. However, an inverse relationship appeared between shrew body mass and mass-specific food and energy utilisation: the largest Eurasian water shrew utilised the least food mass and the least energy quantity per 1 g of its body.

Under laboratory conditions, shrews display some preferences for more profitable prey (in the sense of net energy gain per unit of handling time, and in respect to predation and competition avoidance), especially when they have enough time for foraging and the encounter rate of prey is high. However, even when there is very good prey availability, they display (as many other animals do) partial preferences, i.e. they take more of the most profitable prey, but do not ignore other prey. However, they are selective from the very beginning of a foraging period. And most interestingly, shrews seem to change their prey preferences according to the situation or stage of foraging.

Photo 19.1. The pygmy shrew, the smallest mammal in Białowieża Forest and whole of Poland, eats up to 300% of its body mass per day when nursing its offspring. Photo by Paweł Fabijański.

In the first stage of foraging (searching for prey), shrews tend to prefer big prey. They detect and attack more large prey, while abandoning more smaller ones. This may be dependent on two factors: detection abilities and searching technique. When attacking, shrews also select large prey first and in higher proportions than small prey. This fits in with the optimal foraging theory, which states the largest prey yields the highest energetic gain per unit of handling time, especially for larger shrews. This tendency is stronger if prey availability is low and if shrews forage under insufficient cover. Moreover, this preference suggests that shrews try to shorten foraging time to avoid or minimise the risk of predation and contact with competitors.

Some shrews are expected to display more clearly this preference. These are the few venomous species, including the two water shrew species living in Białowieża Forest. Their venom facilitates the overpowering of especially large prey, including small vertebrates (Photo 19.2). Moreover, by paralysing large prey with venom, water shrews decrease the energy invested in struggling during the attack and further manipulations. Thus, their feeding on large prey can be less costly than for other predators of comparable size.

Shrews select prey also according to their nutritional value. For example, in one experiment, pygmy shrews ate almost exclusively mealworms and fly larvae, which yield a lot of energy and contain little water and indigestible cuticle. It seems that pygmy shrews reduce their total mass of consumed food by eating prey of better

Photo 19.2. Eurasian water shrew with large prey – a small frog. Photo by Grzegorz Okołów.

quality. In contrast, insect larvae composed only 33 to 49% of food eaten by the three other species. For example, common shrews ate many earthworms and amber snails, which contain relatively little energy and a great deal of soil in their guts and water in their bodies.

Both terrestrial and semi-aquatic species of shrews prepare larder stores as well as temporal scattered stores. Larder stores help them survive long periods of low prey availability, as in winter. Scattered hoarding helps shrews maximise their energy net gain and minimise predation risk. It also reduces both intra- and interspecific competition for food by increasing the dispersion of prey and thereby making them more difficult for potential competitors to locate and steal.

Scattered food hoarding by shrews depends on many factors. Usually, shrews intensify food hoarding when there is an over-abundance of prey and their hunger is low. The presence of natural shelters, dispersed within shrew home ranges, promotes scattered hoarding and food consumption in hiding-places far from their nests. Lack of such structures forces shrews to carry food to or near the nest and prepare larder stores.

If the probability of stealing prey from stores is high, the tendency to hoard decreases, even in gregarious species such as the Mediterranean water shrew. For example, when foraging individually, these shrews consumed only few food portions at the sites of finding, and hoarded most food in their nest and/or in hiding-places. During group foraging, the shrews did not hoard food communally, and preparation of individual stores almost ceased. Instead, the shrews immediately consumed most food on the spot.

The proportion of food hoarded by shrews decreased with increasing body size: the smallest pygmy shrew hid proportionally the greatest amount of food, and the largest Eurasian water shrew hid the least amount (Figure 19.1 left). Shrews hoard proportionally more large prey than small prey in both scattered and larder stores. These experiments also revealed that the size of prey hoarded by the shrews was larger than the size of prey eaten (Figure 19.1 right). In addition, large prey was hoarded first and smaller prey later, if ever. Usually, small prey was eaten at once at the finding site. For example, water shrews hoarded large prey such as fish, frogs and snails, whereas they ate immediately small crustaceans (e.g. freshwater hog louses and shrimps), fly larvae, and beetle larvae.

During the utilisation of hoarded prey, shrews display an inverse preference: they eat more small than large prey. How can this be explained? When prey is abundant or easily accessible, the costs of searching and capture are low. These costs are minimal, if any, during utilisation of stores. Therefore, ease of manipulation is a major factor in prey selection. Apparently, small prey is easier to manipulate and bite, which shortens the handling time per one item. In contrast, long and resilient earthworms (left in stores by most shrews) could require a high dexterity in prey handling. Amber snails (hoarded in high proportions by the Mediterranean water shrew) could require a high bite force because of their hard shells. Fish (sticklebacks and small roaches kept in stores by both water shrew species) could be difficult to digest because of their bones. Even if consumption of small prey does not yield maximal energy gains, it can well enough satisfy food needs, which fits the so-called "concept of satisfication". In other words, when shrews are safe in their shelters, they can indulge in some freedom and a decrease of foraging efficiency. In this context, the behaviour of pygmy shrews is especially interesting. These shrews hoarded and ate almost exclusively small prey such as larvae of flies and mealworms. Nevertheless, they chose smaller larvae for eating than for hoarding (Figure 19.1 right). This shows how subtle the mechanisms of prey size selection are.

We can conclude that for hungry, but non-starved shrews, the most effective foraging strategy is the quick hunting of a few large prey, and eating them in a shelter, rather than the time-consuming and risky collection of a number of small prey. Preparing short-term stores is energetically profitable, especially for small species of shrews, because they are unable to store large reserves of energy in their body.

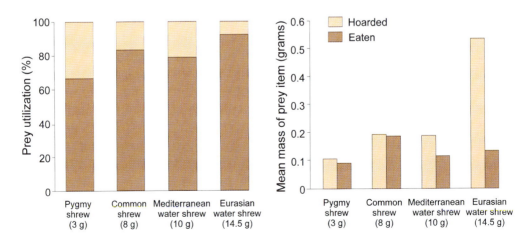

Figure 19.1. Prey eaten versus hoarded in relation to body masses of the four shrew species. (Reprinted from: *Behavioral Ecology* 13: 216–223, 2002; modified.)

Segregation of niches

Two or more species can co-exist for a long time if they differ in at least one niche dimension. These dimensions are, for example, food, habitat, and time of activity. Differentiation of circadian activity is an effective mechanism diminishing interspecific competition among animals. Is this also the case for shrews? Live-trapping and radio-telemetric tracking showed that all shrew species were most active between 20:00 a 1:00 hours, and least active during midday (10:00–15:00; Figure 19.2). However, activity of pygmy and common shrews was significantly lower than that of the two water shrew species in the period 20:00–1:00, whereas their activity was higher in the period 15:00–20:00. Both water shrews clearly displayed a nocturnal, unimodal pattern of circadian activity. In contrast, the activity of pygmy and common shrews was more evenly distributed over 24 hours and can be classified as an all-hours pattern of circadian activity. This was especially true for common shrews. Moreover, terrestrial shrews increased their activity earlier (after 15:00) than water shrews (after 20:00). Generally, however, overlaps of temporal niches of particular species were high (from 75% to over 90%). This suggests that other mechanisms help separate the ecological niches of these species.

Five main foraging modes have been described for shrews: (1) hunting on the ground surface, (2) rooting for prey under the ground surface, (3) climbing on objects such as plants, bushes or rocks, (4)

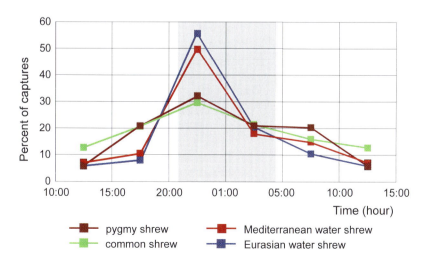

Figure 19.2. Comparison of circadian activity rhythms of the four shrew species co-existing in wet habitats of Białowieża Forest (June/July).

diving for prey in deep water, and (5) wading in shallow water and muddy ground. Certain differentiations among foraging modes were also found within the shrew community in Białowieża Forest. Common shrews foraged mainly in litter and the upper layer of soil (rooting), whereas pygmy shrews foraged on the ground surface and climbed low vegetation. Mediterranean water shrews could only forage successfully in shallow water (wading), whereas Eurasian water shrews were able to forage in both deep (diving) and shallow water (wading). However, both species of water shrews were able to use surface hunting and rooting foraging modes.

Some characteristics of aquatic foraging and diving abilities of the Eurasian water shrew, as revealed in laboratory experiments and field observations, are important in this context. Aquatic prey composes at least 50% of the diet of this species and may reach 95%. Swimming and diving make-up only 5% of its daily activity and usually take place in water not exceeding 30 cm of depth. However, during foraging under laboratory conditions, the Eurasian water shrew dived frequently (up to 890 dives per day) and to considerable depths (over 2 meters). Two different tactics of hunting under water have been described for this species. Pelagic fish (bleak and leucaspius fish) are caught during straight-line swimming in the upper and middle layers of water. After a shoal of small fish is detected, these shrews make sudden head movements and bends of the body to catch a fish by its tail or back. Whereas, bottom fish (tench and gudgeon) and benthic invertebrates are caught by "creeping" on the bottom and "feeling" the surface with their snout. During this type of hunting, Eurasian water shrews frequently change their direction of movement and stop. They then dig with their snout and forefeet, squeezing under stones and other objects lying on the bottom, and turning them up. This results in a thorough searching of the streambed.

Shrews often display high levels of interspecific overlap of habitat niches, especially in wet habitats, which are the most productive in terms of biomass and density of prey. In Białowieża Forest, such habitats exist in the river valleys. In the Narewka river valley, microhabitat selection in the four species of shrews was studied by live-trapping and radio-telemetry, accompanied by a detailed analysis of habitat. Distance to the stream and ground wetness appeared to be more important than plant cover type in segregation of shrew habitat niches (Figure 19.3). The Eurasian water shrew occupied places significantly wetter and closer to streams than the three other species. It preferred sites with direct access to streams with deep water and steep, structured banks. The

Mediterranean water shrew preferred sites wetter and closer to streams than the common shrew. This water shrew selected places at some distance from streams, flooded with shallow or medium water, covered by dense sedges and close to trees. The Eurasian water shrew tended also to prefer open habitats (such as sedge-swamps and marshy meadows), in contrast to the tendency of the Mediterranean water shrew to prefer more closed habitats (ecotones and forests). Finally, the pygmy shrew lived closer to streams than the common shrew. These microhabitat differences are related to different foraging modes of the four species (Figure 19.3). Thus, the habitat preferences of shrews reflect vertical segregation in their foraging microhabitats.

The largest Eurasian water shrew had the narrowest habitat niche, the smallest pygmy shrew displayed the broadest niche, and the medium-sized species – intermediate niches. Interestingly, trophic niche breadths of these species change in the opposite direction: from the broadest in Eurasian water shrews to the narrowest in pygmy shrews. This can be explained in the following way: a trophic generalist, which is able to eat a variety of prey

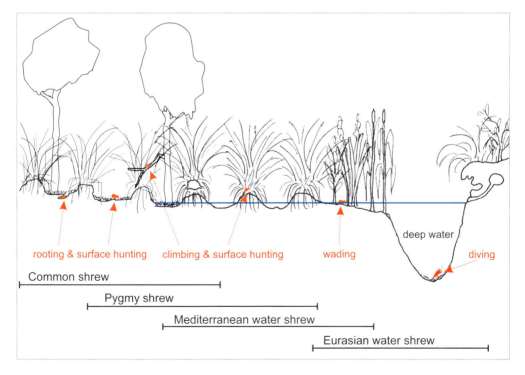

Figure 19.3. Vertical segregation of microhabitat niches of the four shrew species based on their different foraging modes. (Reprinting from: *Säugetierkundliche Informationen* 5(25): 99–112. 2001; modified.)

(terrestrial and aquatic, small and large), can satisfy its food requirements within a small area and few habitats. Thus, Eurasian water shrews, living along stream banks, have simultaneous access to both aquatic and terrestrial resources and are not obliged to utilise other habitats. In contrast, a trophic specialist, such as the pygmy shrew, is only able to utilise small surface prey and has to search for its specific food over a larger area and in a greater variety of habitats. In fact, Eurasian water shrews have much smaller home ranges (200–400 m^2) than pygmy shrews (900–1800 m^2).

In conclusion, the separation of ecological niches in the shrew community (that in Białowieża Forest and perhaps in many other communities in the Holarctic) is achieved by differentiation of both microhabitats and trophic niches, based on differences in body size and morphological adaptations. Patterns of circadian activity seem to be less important.

Investigations of shrew communities revealed many complex and subtle biological and ecological mechanisms of avoiding intra- and interspecific competition. Unfortunately, the best habitats for shrews – swamps, wet meadows, streams and small rivers – are gradually disappearing from European landscapes due to human pressure. As a result, there are not many regions left in Poland and the whole of Europe, where multi-species guilds of shrews still survive.

Suggested readings

Churchfield S. 1990. The natural history of shrews. Christopher Helm, Bromley.

Rychlik L. 1997. Differences in foraging behaviour between water shrews: *Neomys anomalus* and *Neomys fodiens*. Acta Theriologica 42: 351–386.

Rychlik L. 1998. Evolution of social systems in shrews. [In: Evolution of shrews. J. M. Wójcik and M. Wolsan, eds]. Mammal Research Institute, Białowieża: 347–406.

Rychlik L. 2000. Habitat preferences of four sympatric species of shrews. Acta Theriologica 45, Suppl. 1: 173–190.

Rychlik L. and Jancewicz E. 2002. Prey size, prey nutrition, and food handling by shrews of different body sizes. Behavioural Ecology 13: 216–223.

20

Common shrews
– chromosome races and evolution

Jan Marek Wójcik

Common shrews are among the most widespread mammals in Eurasia. What can be so exciting in studying common shrews? Surprisingly, the answer is: their chromosomes. They have one of the most variable karyotypes of all mammalian species. Such variability fascinates biologists because chromosomal rearrangements (mutations) can lead to the evolution of new species.

Chromosome races

Intraspecific (within-species) chromosome variation is not rare among mammals. Yet the common shrew, which occurs in many habitats throughout Eurasia shows phenomenal variability in this respect (Photo 20.1). Karyotypic variation of the Robertsonian type is associated with whole-arm chromosome rearrangements. Whole-arm chromosome mutations change the number of chromosomes, but not the number of chromosome arms in the karyotype. In the common shrew the diploid number of chromosomes varies within the species from 20 to 33, whereas the number of chromosome arms remains constant at 40 (Figure 20.1). Also, the sex chromosome system in this species, as well as seven related species of shrews, is unusual: it is XY_1Y_2 in the male karyotype and XX in the female one.

The chromosomal variation of common shrews has been studied in detail throughout Eurasia. Comparisons with other species of shrews indicate that the ancestral karyotype of the common shrew

Photo 20.1. A common shrew and its chromosomes. Photos by Paweł Fabijański and Jan M. Wójcik.

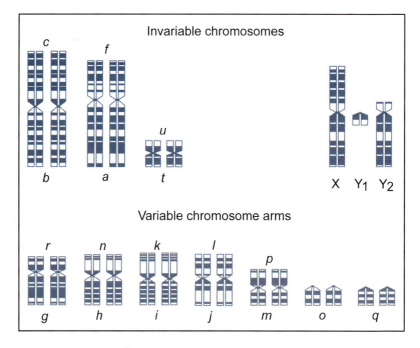

Figure 20.1. Diagram of G-banded karyotype of the Białowieża race of the common shrew, documented from eastern Poland. Each substantial chromosome arm is denoted by a lower-case letter with a being the largest. Three pairs of bi-armed autosomes (metacentrics), af, bc and tu, are invariant, whereas autosomal arms g–r can occur as single-armed chromosomes (acrocentrics) and/or combine together as different metacentrics.

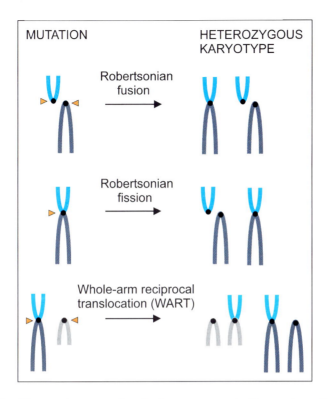

Figure 20.2. Three types of whole-arm mutations in chromosomes. Robertsonian fusion joins together two single-armed (ie. acrocentric) chromosomes at their centromeres to form a single bi-armed (ie. metacentric) chromosome. The fission is a reverse process. Whole-arm reciprocal translocations (WART) occur between a metacentric and an acrocentric or between two metacentrics. Arrowheads indicate breakpoints. (Reprinted from: *Evolution of Shrews*. Mammal Research Institute, Białowieża, pp. 219–268, 1998.)

consisted of single-armed chromosomes. This karyotype evolved into numerous chromosome races thanks to Robertsonian fusions and/or whole-arm reciprocal translocations (Figure 20.2). In karyotypes among different races of this species, chromosome arms *g–r* (see Figure 20.1) can form a total of 38 different bi-armed chromosomes (Figure 20.3).

So far, sixty-eight different chromosome races have been described in the common shrew throughout Eurasia (Figure 20.4). A chromosome race is a group of geographically contiguous or recently separated populations which share the same set of metacentrics and acrocentrics by descent. The name of a race usually comes from a neighbouring town, distinct geographical feature, or the province or region where it was first described. In Poland alone, eleven races have been identified.

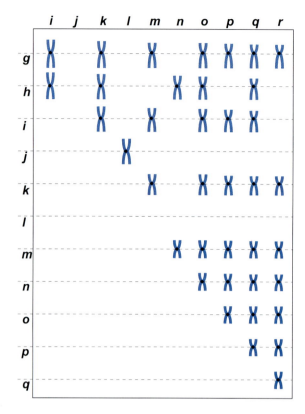

Figure 20.3. Various bi-armed chromosomes found in common shrew populations in Eurasia. (Reprinted from: *Mammalia* 66: 169–178, 2003.)

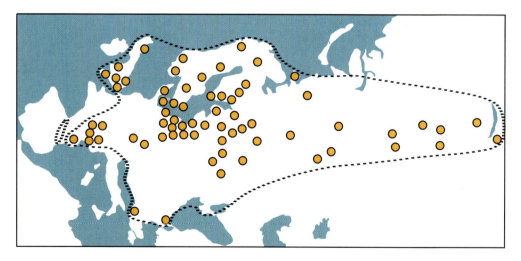

Figure 20.4. Description sites of 68 chromosome races of the common shrew in Eurasia. Dotted line indicates the approximate geographic range of the species. (Reprinted from: *Mammalia* 66: 169–178, 2003; modified.)

A phylogenetic analysis identified four karyotypic groups in the common shrew: the West European, North European, East European and Siberian. Bi-armed chromosomes with an arm *g* or *h* are particularly important in defining these groups. Chromosomes *gk*, *gm*, *go*, and *gr* are very widespread (Figure 20.5). This is intriguing because arms *g* and *h* are the largest among those that show Robertsonian variation. Evolutionarily, it seems that the first autosomal bi-armed chromosomes formed by arm fusions were *af* and *bc*. Then, the medium-sized chromosome *jl* evolved, followed by various chromosomes containing arms *g*, *h* and *i*. Bi-armed chromosomes with at least one large or medium-sized autosomal acrocentric are more likely to arise and become fixed in a shrew population.

As described above, chromosome races differ in their composition of acrocentrics and metacentrics. What is more, Robertsonian polymorphism occurs within the populations. In such cases, twin acrocentric and metacentric morphs (and simple Robertsonian heterozygotes) of particular chromosome pairs may occur within one population. Such polymorphism was frequently found in hybrid zones between different races. There are also examples of polymorphic populations that do not occur in a hybrid zone: for instance on the island of Islay (United Kingdom), on Öland Island in the Baltic Sea (Sweden), and in Białowieża Primeval Forest (Poland).

There are different hypotheses explaining polymorphism in non-hybrid-zone populations. One claims that polymorphism represents the 'ghost of hybridization past'. Past hybridization events may

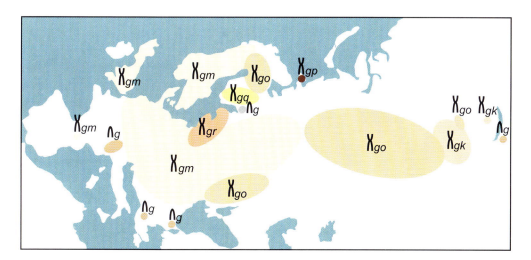

Figure 20.5. Schematic ranges of chromosomes involving the arm *g* in the common shrew from Eurasia. (Reprinted from: *Acta Theriologica* 47: 139–167, 2002; modified.)

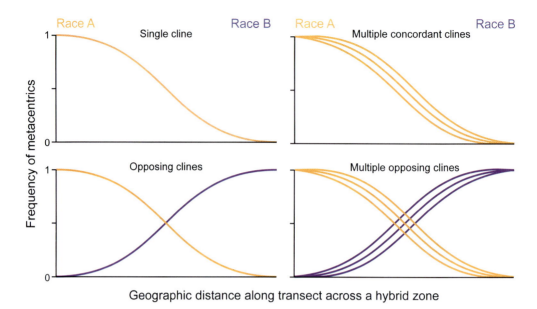

Figure 20.6. Various types of metacentric clines in hybrid zones between different chromosomal races of the common shrew. (Reprinted from: *Evolution of Shrew*s. Mammal Research Institute, Białowieża, pp. 219–268, 1998; modified.)

have generated long-lasting polymorphism by colonization processes. Shrews that initially colonized different parts of the current species range may have derived from hybrid zones and then polymorphism may have become widely spread. Another possible explanation is that polymorphism occurs as a result of new chromosome mutations. Finally, such polymorphism could have been caused by either past hybridization events or new mutations, but is now maintained by natural selection.

Interestingly, the extraordinary chromosomal subdivision of the common shrew is not mirrored by diversity in its allozymes and DNA sequences. Studies of allozyme variation revealed little genic differentiation between chromosome races in Great Britain, Poland and Sweden. Although there are no diagnostic alleles, the differences in allele frequencies at some loci (particularly at a locus of mannose phosphate isomerase) suggest that gene flow between some races may be restricted. On the other hand, in Poland the variation of mitochondrial DNA haplotypes in the common shrew is relatively high in some races but the nucleotide diversity is low. This means the common shrew is not a particularly inbred animal, nor can inbreeding explain its chromosome variation.

Thus, what can explain the lack of significant differentiation in mtDNA or allozymes between populations of common shrews?

Probably it was caused by the rapid radiation of one or more poorly differentiated source population(s) into different geographic regions. In Poland, the study of mtDNA in common shrews seems to support this hypothesis.

Hybrid zones of races

A hybrid zone is an area of occurrence where Robertsonian heterozygotes differ from the two out-zone races. There is extraordinary variety in the types of hybrid zones where common shrew races occur. All the basic structures that might be expected on secondary contact of either a metacentric race and an acrocentric race or two metacentric races have been observed. Therefore, different metacentric clines can be formed in such zones, respectively: single or multiple concordant clines and opposing or multiple opposing clines (Figure 20.6).

The simplest situation of a single cline occurs in various parts of the common shrew's range. It happens, for instance, when race A has a metacentric chromosome not existing in race B. The frequency of the metacentric chromosome within their contact (hybrid) zone gradually decreases towards the race B (see Figure 20.6). In such hybrid zones, the area of polymorphism is wide (about 100 km) and there is a smooth gradient in the frequency of single metacentrics going from one pure race to the other. Examples of such hybrid zones have been observed in England. If one of the races has several metacentrics not found in the other, the hybrid zone consists of multiple concordant metacentric clines, and the area of polymorphism is also wide. Such a hybrid zone was found in the Czech Republic.

Opposing metacentric clines are expected when a race with a bi-armed chromosome comes into contact with a race characterised by other metacentrics (Figure 20.6). Zones of this type have been documented in England, Sweden, Poland, and Russia (Siberia). The clines that make up multiple opposing zones are much narrower than those found in the two former types of hybrids. This probably reflects greater selection against complex heterozygotes, as heterozygous shrews may be less fit than homozygous ones.

Two interesting modifications were observed in some of the hybrid zones between chromosome races: an acrocentric peak and a recombinant peak. The acrocentric peak was formed when there was a high frequency of individuals with acrocentrics (homologous to the metacentrics that comprise the opposing clines) in the centre of the hybrid zone. The recombinant peak was formed when a high frequency of individuals, homozygous for metacentrics that define opposing clines, occurred in the centre of the hybrid zone. It might be expected that natural selection would favour the evolution of hybrid zones with acrocentric and recombinant peaks. The presence of such peaks reduces the frequency of complex heterozygotes with low fitness.

Gene flow across chromosomal hybrid zones in common shrews was studied by genetic markers such as allozymes, DNA microsatellites and the mitochondrial cytochrome b gene. Interestingly, chromosomal hybrid zones in this species appeared to be rather weak barriers to gene flow. Indeed, a study on allozyme loci in Poland revealed that gene flow in a hybrid zone with a recombinant peak was not seriously restricted.

Nevertheless, there are some indications that present-day gene flow among particular races could be limited. Studies of mtDNA, in populations of different races in Poland, showed most individuals had unique haplotypes that were not observed elsewhere. Moreover, the distribution of the most common haplotype was limited to only three out of ten studied populations of shrews.

Chromosomal evolution

An intriguing question in chromosomal evolution of the common shrew is: Where were the refugia from which the species expanded at the end of the last glaciation and early post-glacial period (ca 15,000–7,000 BP)? Chromosomal data obtained from different populations in Eurasia suggest that shrews currently occupying central and northern Europe originated from several "refugial" populations. These parts of Europe were probably colonized primarily from the Iberian and Balkan regions (Figure 20.7). However, shrew populations in Finland and western Siberia might have derived from a glacial refugium in the southern Urals. A still different situation could have occurred on the Italian peninsula where some populations of shrews were likely not able to spread north of the Alps. They may have been geographically isolated for a long period of time, accumulating new mutations in mtDNA sequence and chromosome rearrangements.

The ancestral karyotype for the common shrew was most probably acrocentric. Besides the Robertsonian fusions leading to a metacentric state, there is also a possibility of whole-arm reciprocal translocations generating new metacentrics (see Figure 20.2). The distribution and chromosomal relationships of some races in Finland,

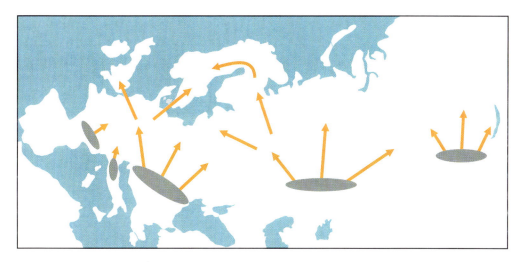

Figure 20.7. Possible routes of post-glacial expansion of the common shrew. Shaded areas indicate refugial populations. (Based on Fig. 3 in *Russian Journal of Genetics* 37: 351–357, 2001; modified.)

Sweden and western Siberia can be explained by stepwise whole-arm reciprocal translocations along a geographical sequence of races.

Concerning chromosomal evolution in the common shrew, three facts are certain: (1) The presence of chromosomal mutations; (2) Local fixation of chromosomal variants; and (3) In some cases, a wider spread of the variants. New chromosome mutations (such as those of the Robertsonian type) are generally expected to be lost from populations. Theoretical studies suggested that such mutations could be fixed either by strong deterministic processes (selection or meiotic drive) or as a result of small population size (due to genetic drift or inbreeding in small, isolated populations). If chromosomal variants are generated at a reasonable rate in small populations, fixation by genetic drift seems inevitable. Although nowadays, in favourable habitats common shrews exist in large continuous populations, in the past the population structure of the species might have been different. It is, however, doubtful that genetic drift alone generated so many fixations. Probably, Robertsonian fusions have some sort of selective advantage, which increases the chance of fixation.

Chromosomal races of the common shrew evolved during the last glacial period and spread during the process of post-glacial recolonization. Thus, chromosomal evolution has been extremely rapid. Molecular data (cytochrome *b* gene) from common shrews in western Europe supported the hypothesis of the migration of metacentrics through acrocentric populations and the recent origin of Robertsonian variation in this karyotypic group. Furthermore, the diversity of mitochondrial DNA of the common shrew in Poland testifies the recent origin of its chromosomal variability.

If the concept of chromosomal speciation is true, great chromosomal differences should promote the creation of new species. Indeed, one of the chromosome races of the common shrew from Switzerland (the Valais race) was recently promoted to the species rank and named *Sorex antinorii* (now regarded as a sibling species of the common shrew). The karyotype of this new shrew species is characterized by the metacentrics *hj* and *lo*, and forms a sister group to all chromosome races of the common shrew. It probably survived on the Italian peninsula during the last glaciation and had a long period of independent evolution. The Valais shrew, *Sorex antinorii*, occuring in southern Switzerland and Italy is karyologically, morphologically, biochemically, and genetically distinct from all known chromosome races of the common shrew.

Despite its uniqueness, the chromosome variation observed in shrews in not the only case among mammals. Similar variation has been found in the house mouse suggesting that chromosomal rearrangements might be frequent. These cases certainly contribute to better understanding of evolution and speciation in mammals.

Suggested readings

Ratkiewicz M., Fedyk S., Banaszek A., Chętnicki W., Szałaj K., Gielly L. and Taberlet P. 2002. The evolutionary history of the two karyotypic groups of the common shrew, *Sorex araneus*, in Poland. Heredity 88: 235–242.

Searle J. B. and Wójcik J. M. 1998. Chromosomal evolution: the case of *Sorex araneus*. [In: Evolution of shrews. J. M. Wójcik and M. Wolsan, eds.] Mammal Research Institute PAS Białowieża: 219–268.

Wójcik J. M., Borodin P. M., Fedyk S., Fredga K., Hausser J., Mishta A., Orlov V. N., Searle J. B., Volobouev V. T. and Zima J. 2003. The list of chromosome races of the common shrew *Sorex araneus* (updated 2002). Mammalia 68:169–178.

Wójcik J. M., Ratkiewicz M. and Searle J. B. 2002. Evolution of the common shrew, *Sorex araneus*: chromosomal and molecular aspects. Acta Theriologica 47, Suppl. 1: 139–167.

Wójcik J. M. and Searle J. B. 1988. The chromosome complement of *Sorex granarius* – the ancestral karyotype of the common shrew (*Sorex araneus*)? Heredity 61: 225–229.

21

Genetic diversity of mammals

Małgorzata Tokarska, Anna M. Wójcik
and Jan M. Wójcik

A bison and a deer look so different that we do not need to analyse their DNA to prove that they differ. But when examining a herd of bison without using a molecular approach, we are unable to guess whether they are related or not, nor how genetically different they are. Here is a brief description of how biologists study the genetic diversity of species, and what the results of such studies can tell us about animals.

Genetic ABC

The source of all forms of inherited diversity in living creatures is their genetic variability. Although the term 'genetic variability' refers to protein or DNA (deoxyribonucleic acid) variability, we should remember that protein variability originates from the multiformity of a DNA sequence. DNA carries all the genetic information of an individual. The deoxyribonucleic acid is a biopolymer, consisting of two linear, unbranched strands of nucleotides (Figure 21.1). Each nucleotide contains a sugar-deoxyribose, a base (purine or pyrimidine) and a phosphate group. Bases of the opposite strands are bound by hydrogen bonds, always forming complementary base pairs: thymine (T) with adenine (A), and cytosine (C) with guanine (G). There are two types of DNA in animals: nuclear, or so-called genomic DNA, and mitochondrial DNA. Both molecules can provide information for genetic diversity surveys.

Nuclear DNA consists of coding and non-coding fragments. Coding sequences, or genes contain instructions for RNA (ribonucleic acid) or protein synthesis. DNA variability in genes may result in differences of protein sequences and thus can alter its spatial structure and function. A "polymorphic" gene has more than one variant in a population. Most of the known genes are polymorphic and this may result in polymorphism of the proteins they code for. But proteins polymorphism is only a small part of DNA polymorphism. Actually, far more important in genetic studies is the polymorphism of non-coding fragments of nuclear DNA. They are called "junk-DNA" but they are not useless. They constitute about 95% of all nuclear DNA and contain regulatory sequences for gene expression, protein synthesis and DNA replication and other sequences of different origin. There is a hypothesis that junk DNA is a potential basis for evolution. Thus, it is extremely informative when studying the genetic diversity of a population.

The nuclear genome contains certain sequences called mini-satellites and microsatellites that are very helpful when genetically

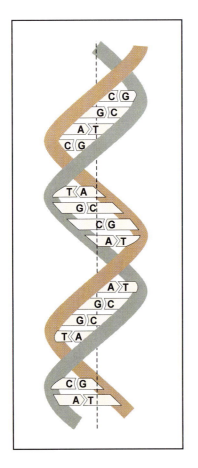

Figure 21.1. DNA structure. Subsequent nucleotides in a DNA strand are recorded as a row of letters referring to respective bases, e.g. TCGACAGCTAGA TTTCCAGGCTGGAATCCTGCC.

profiling a population. Minisatellites (VNTR – Variable Number of Tandem Repeats) are repeats of quite long (tens of nucleotides) sequences with a high repeat number variation, making them very informative. Unfortunately, they are not widely spread through the genome and may be problematic in analysis due to their length. DNA microsatellites have become a key tool in studies on genomes of many species. Microsatellites are short, usually dinucleotide repeats in the nuclear DNA (Figure 21.2), present throughout the genome. Although their sites are species specific (e.g. each red deer individual has microsatellite sequences at the very same sites), their length (number of dinucleotide repeats) is extremely variable among individuals. Thus, if sufficient numbers of microsatellites are analysed, they create a unique pattern for each animal (Figure 21.2). A fingerprint pattern based on DNA microsatellites does not change during the individual's lifetime and thus can be a basis for precise individual identification.

Mitochondrial DNA (mtDNA) is also used in genetic studies. Mitochondria are thought to be descendants of alpha-proteobacteria

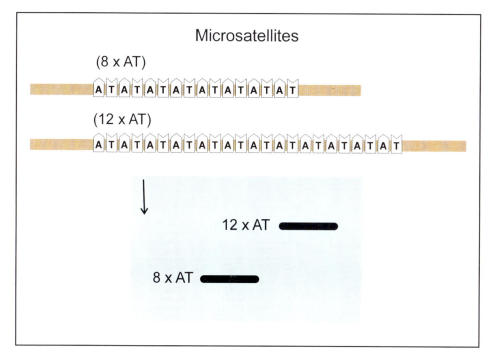

Figure 21.2. Microsatellites are short, usually dinucleotide repeats in the nuclear DNA (top). Different lengths of the respective DNA microsatellite sequences result in distinct band patterns on the electrophoretic gel (bottom). They produce a unique 'DNA fingerprint' pattern for an individual. The arrow indicates the direction of migration of DNA fragments.

that once became endosymbionts. As a result, bacterial and mitochondrial DNA are similar and both differ markedly from eukaryotic nuclear DNA. The mitochondrial genome is maternally inherited *via* the egg cell. Mitochondrial DNA is short, circular and hardly contains any non-coding sequences. It contains genes coding for ribosomal RNA, transporter RNA and enzymes of OXPHOS (oxidative phosphorylation). Although their sequences are conservative, mtDNA mutates up to 17 times faster than nuclear DNA. Additionally, these mutations (evolutionary changes in DNA structure) in the mitochondrial genome are not repairable, thus they accumulate quickly. These factors make mtDNA a source of valuable data for phylogenetic and evolutionary studies.

Both nuclear microsatellites and mtDNA analysis may be used in various assays: for estimation of genetic distance, relationship analysis, inter- and intrapopulation differentiation, evolutionary studies on the pace and directions of genetic structural changes, and for building phylogenetic trees. Microsatellites are also the main tool in individual identification assays and pedigree control. MtDNA is not used in the two latter analyses for two reasons: it is only maternally inherited and may change during an individual's lifetime.

Know-how

Electrophoresis, a standard technique in polymorphism analyses, is a method to visibly separate nucleic acids or proteins. With this

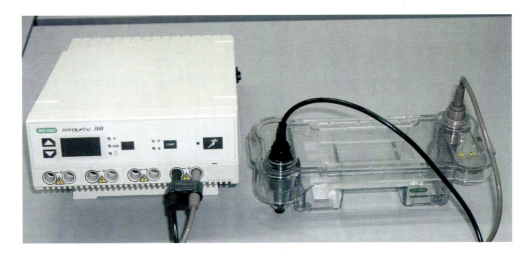

Photo 21.1. A simple electrophoretic set consisting of a power supply (left) and a gel unit (right). Photo by Małgorzata Tokarska.

procedure, it is possible to identify protein molecules that differ by a single amino acid and DNA fragments that vary by as little as one nucleotide. Only the newest technical achievement of DNA analysis (Real-time PCR) limited, though did not replace, the ubiquitous necessity of electrophoresis as a readout tool.

Electrophoresis separates molecules (proteins or nucleic acids) by their size and electricity. Longer molecules have difficulty in moving through the porous gel, and hence cannot migrate as rapidly as the smaller ones. Molecules with negative electric charge migrate towards the anode (+), while positively charged molecules move towards the cathode (–). Proteins may have different electrical charges but DNA has a negative charge, thus it always moves towards the anode. Agarose and polyacrylamide are the media most frequently used for preparing electrophoresis gels.

A typical electrophoretical set consists of a power supply of appropriate voltage and a gel container, in which the gel is poured, samples are applied, and divisions run (Photo 21.1). After division, the separated macromolecules can usually be seen as a series of bands or peaks spread from one end of the gel to the other. Protein electrophoresis had long been the major method to analyse biodiversity (Figure 21.3). It can be used to determine the genetic

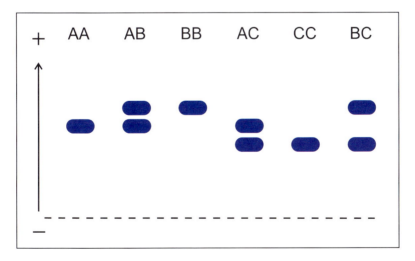

Figure 21.3. An example of electrophoretic patterns obtained for monomeric protein (in this case: mannose phosphate isomerase) in the common shrew. Bands represent particular alleles (A, B, C) and allow identification of homozygous (AA, BB, CC) and hetorozygous (AB, AC, BC) individuals in the study samples. The dashed line shows the sample origin and the arrow indicates direction of migration.

differences within and among populations and the evolutionary relationship between species.

DNA is located in the nucleus of a cell, and before analysis it must be extracted and isolated. Contemporary methods have enabled DNA to be obtained from any kind of tissue, even archaeological, decayed or trace materials. For years, the main problem in DNA assays was the limited amount of isolated molecules that could be extracted for analysis. This problem had been solved by the mid 1980's, when the new era in nucleic acid biology began. PCR (Polymerase Chain Reaction), a method of unlimited DNA replication was a revolution in molecular biology (Figure 21.4). PCR mimes *in vivo* DNA replication, effectively multiplying DNA fragments even from a single initial molecule in less than a few hours. PCR is a multiple repetition of a thermal cycle, doubling the amount of DNA in each cycle. The reaction is performed in small volumes, in a vial containing polymerase enzymes, free nucleotides, initial DNA molecules (matrix), a reaction buffer, and primers. PCR cannot amplify the entire genomic DNA, due to its length, hence fragments need to be selected beforehand. The chosen regions are flanked by primers, DNA oligonucleotides usually with a short sequence of 10–25 base pairs, so they can then be selectively amplified (Figure 21.4).

PCR is a fundamental tool for common population genetics assays, such as DNA fingerprinting and DNA sequencing. DNA fingerprinting is the general term used for individual identification methods, based on the uniqueness of a DNA pattern. DNA fingerprinting usually relies on DNA microsatellite analyses, but can also

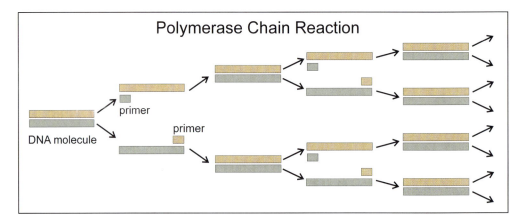

Figure 21.4. A simple scheme of Polymerase Chain Reaction (PCR), which allows a rapid and effective replication of DNA. After 30 cycles there is approximately 2^{30} DNA molecules in a PCR vial out of one initial molecule.

be performed using other techniques. An RFLP assay (Restriction Fragment Length Polymorphism) for example, uses restriction enzymes that cut genomic DNA at the enzyme-specific sites, producing unique patterns of restriction fragments. DNA fingerprinting is used in a variety of biological diversity studies, for identification, pedigree analyses, reproductive success, molecular evolution, and phylogeny.

Mitochondrial DNA does not contain microsatellite sequences. MtDNA includes a hypervariable region (the so-called D-Loop), which is the target for most molecular approaches. The D-Loop region mutates even faster than the rest of the mtDNA, and the most effective way of tracing these mutations is to use DNA sequencing. Sequencing of DNA is an extremely sensitive technique, that identifies, step by step, each nucleotide of a chosen, previously amplified fragment. It 'catches' all the differences in DNA structure, even those omitted by other, less accurate techniques.

Regardless of the DNA fingerprinting technique used, a series of bands or peaks on electrophoretical gel is obtained. Figure 21.5

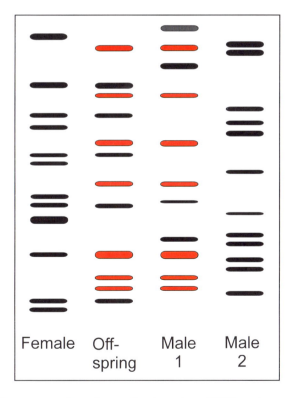

Figure 21.5. An example of reading out a DNA microsatellite electrophoretogram in pedigree control. Patterns of bands shown in the figure exclude paternity of male 2. Red-coloured bands suggest that male 1 is the father of the descendant.

shows an example of paternity identification using DNA patterns (bands). When reading an electrophoretogram to assert a pedigree, one feature at least must be observed. Each marker (DNA microsatellite) in the descendant's DNA pattern must be present in either of the parents' samples. If not, it leads to the exclusion of one or both parents from the pedigree.

Applications

Genetic analyses can help find relationships between genotype, phenotype and environmental factors, and can determine relatedness and genetic diversity within or among populations. Molecular biology techniques, especially DNA analyses, can trace the flow of genes in a population and their historical geographical distribution. They are usually the only source of information on the phylogeny of species, based on genetic material of different age and stage of decay.

Studies on genetic polymorphism and diversity conducted by researchers of the Mammal Research Institute PAS in Białowieża, Poland, started in the late 1970's. During the following years, various aspects of genetic diversity in mammals have been investigated.

Studies on allozyme polymorphism in the bank vole population in Białowieża Forest showed that genetic differences were more distinct between seasonal generations than between resident and migrant individuals. A relationship was found between vitality and fertility parameters of bank voles and the serum esterase phenotype,

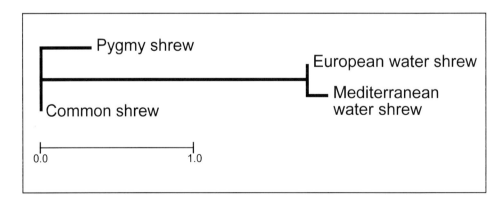

Figure 21.6. An unrooted tree showing the Nei's genetic distances between four species of shrews from Białowieża Forest. Genetic distances were calculated using allele frequencies from 25 enzyme loci. (Reprinted from: *Biochemical Systematics and Ecology* 24: 291–298, 1996; modified.)

with heterozygotes being more fertile and more vital than homozygotes. The mating system and reproductive success of a free-living population of bank voles were determined by mark-recapture and electrophoretic techniques. Furthermore, seasonal changes of transferrin allozyme frequencies were found in a Białowieża population of yellow-necked mice. A significant overabundance of heterozygotes found in springs indicates their better adaptation to winter conditions.

A comparison of electrophoretical mobility of enzymes in four shrew species in Białowieża Forest showed higher mean heterozygosity in the common shrew and European water shrew, than in the pygmy shrew and Mediterranean water shrew. This study enabled phylogenetic trees to be constructed for the four shrew species (Figure 21.6).

Electrophoretical protein studies in common shrews show a possible relationship between allozyme polymorphism and the environmental heterogeneity of Białowieża Forest. A proposed hypothesis suggests that an important factor in sustaining diversity might be the different selection pressures of particular biotopes, while random factors, such as genetic drift may affect allele frequency changes in the population. Another study on chromosome and genetic diversity in the common shrew in Poland revealed that in spite of extremely high chromosome structural diversity, there is practically no significant protein variation within the species.

In regards to the larger mammals, an estimation of allozyme polymorphism in the European bison (Lowland-Białowieża line), the species that had experienced an extreme genetic bottleneck (see Chapter 4), revealed a significant genetic depletion in the free-living herd in Białowieża Forest. Studies on genetic diversity and relatedness within packs of wolves, using both radio-telemetry and DNA microsatellite analysis, allowed genetic diversity to be examined within Białowieża Forest wolf packs, which turned out to be higher than expected. Mitochondrial DNA sequencing in the same study distinguished four mtDNA haplotypes (sets of genes inherited together) in a wolf population of Białowieża Forest.

In the future, both the range of mammalian species studied and the questions asked in the research projects of Mammal Research Institute PAS will broaden. Combining the population genetics approach with the fields of ecology and conservation biology open many new perspectives for a better understanding of the living world.

Suggested readings

Berg P. and Singer M. 1992. Dealing with genes. The language of heredity. University Science Books, Mill Valley, California.

Brown T. A. 1999. Genomes. BIOS Scientific Publishers Limited. Oxford.

Primrose S. B. 1998. Principles of genome analysis: A guide to mapping and sequencing DNA from different organisms. Blackwell Science Limited, Oxford.

Richardson B. J., Baverstock P. R. and Adams M. 1986. Allozyme electrophoresis. A handbook for animal systematics and population studies. Academic Press, Inc. San Diego, California.

Turner P. C., McLennan A. G., Bates A. D. and White M. R. H. 2000. Instant notes in molecular biology (2nd edition). BIOS Scientific Publishers Limited. Oxford.

Wójcik J. M., Wójcik A. M., Zalewska H. and Rychlik L. 1996. Allozyme differentiation in four sympatric species of European shrews (Soricidae: Mammalia). Biochemical Systematics and Ecology 24: 291–298.

22

Morphometrics of mammals – the scientific success of teeth

Elwira Szuma

For many people it will come as a surprise that mammalian teeth have been particularly successful as a subject of scientific enquiry. In palaeontology, teeth play a principal role in our knowledge of evolutionary history. In living populations, tooth traits can reflect their present status, and can also be used to predict evolutionary changes to come.

"Stone" tissue

Without doubt, teeth are the hardest structures in the mammalian body. Covered by a highly mineralised enamel layer, teeth are the most frequently found fossil mammal remains at excavation sites (Photo 22.1). Much of our knowledge of early mammalian evolution is based on studies of fossil teeth. Also, the systematic division of modern mammal taxons is in great part based on various types of dental systems and dental patterns.

Most mammals have heterodont dentition, which consists of teeth that vary in both structure and function. The anteriormost teeth, the incisors and canines, are used to gather or kill food, whereas the more specialised cheek teeth, the premolars and molars, are used to grind or slice food in preparation for digestion. Typically, two sets of teeth appear in a mammal's lifetime. The deciduous dentition, which develops early and includes incisors, canines and premolars, is followed by a second set of teeth that erupt when the

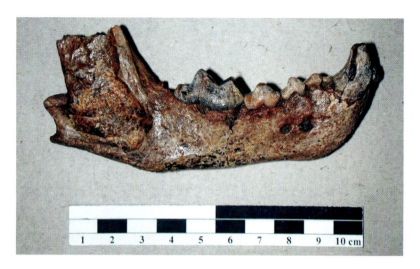

Photo 22.1. Petrified mandible of a wolverine 30,000 year BP. Photo by Piotr Wojtal.

animal matures. This second, permanent dentition consists of molars, in addition to the incisors, canines and premolars. The number of teeth of each type of dentition is represented by a dental formula. This formula varies throughout different systematic groups of mammals. For example, in the red fox it is written as follows: incisors 3/3, canines 1/1, premolars 4/4, and molars 2/3. This score indicates the number of upper and lower teeth on one side of a tooth-row (the jaw). Therefore, the number of teeth in the formula must be doubled to give the total number of teeth in the dentition. In the case of the red fox it would be a total of 42.

Cheek teeth, and in particular molars, are the most interesting part of the dental system in mammals. In most extant mammals, the molars are strictly related to the type of food consumed and the way it is obtained. Regarding the height of teeth, we can recognise mammals with brachydont (short-crowned) and hypsodont (high crowned) teeth. Most mammals have brachydont teeth. Many herbivores, because their teeth are subject to rapid wear, have hypsodont teeth. In some mammals, the further adaptation to abrasive food is ever--growing (hypselodont) teeth.

Considering the shape of the tooth crown, teeth are divided into bunodont, secodont, lophodont or selenodont types (Photo 22.2). The bunodont type is characterised by wide crowns with blunt cusps, separated by shallow grooves. Such teeth, occurring in pigs, some rodents, carnivores, and primates, are adapted to crushing and grinding food. Secodont teeth are observed in many insectivores, bats, and carnivores. These teeth serve to slice food by their op-

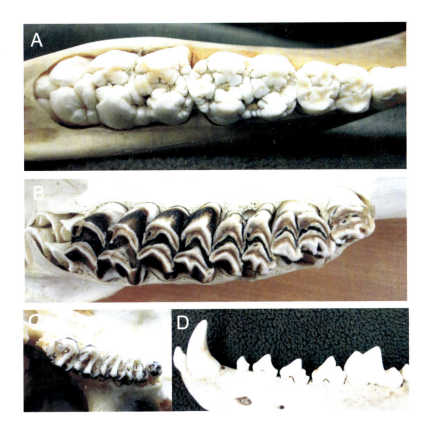

Photo 22.2. Basic dental types in modern mammals: (A) bunodont teeth of a wild boar; (B) selenodont teeth of moose; (C) lophodont teeth of woodchuck; (D) secodont teeth of wolf. Photos by Małgorzata Karczewska.

posing, blade-like edges coming together. One pair of such opposing teeth is particularly specialised and enlarged. These are called the carnassials and consist of the last upper premolar and first lower molar. Herbivorous mammals have to grind large quantities of tough food. Therefore, the crowns are wider and covered by ridges of various shapes. The lophodont type, with cusps forming comparatively straight ridges, is observed in elephants, rhinoceroses, hyraxes, and some rodents. In the selenodont type the cusps form crescents. This dental type occurs in horses, deer, cattle, gazelles, and camels (Photo 22.2).

In some species, tooth number or size differs between sexes. For example, in some deer that have no antlers, the upper canines are much bigger in males than females. Also, differences in tusk development in relation to sex are observed in the Indian elephant: in females the tusks are often absent or very small. Moreover, in many mammalian species, sexual dimorphism in tooth size is observed. In carnivores, and particularly in mustelids, males have bigger teeth than females. Sexual dimorphism in the dental systems of mammals is a behavioural adaptation to different social systems. Wherever males compete for females, teeth may be used as weapons in fights.

Finally, other factors such as evolutionary history, geographic distribution, and ecological conditions play significant roles in shaping the dental patterns within particular populations of species.

What do dental patterns of a red fox tell us?

In the red fox, as in other carnivores, the most important teeth are the carnassials, which perform both grinding and cutting functions. The canines are used to kill prey, and the incisors to catch and hold prey. Premolars and posterior molars play a secondary role in respect to catching and grinding food (Photo 22.3). However, foxes use their teeth not only for eating, but also in social interactions. The canines, for example, serve as weapons between competing males for mates. Measurements of small differences in complexity and size of fox teeth, from 1,500 skulls collected in Poland over a period of 70 years (from 1927 to 1996), have revealed that microevolutionary changes took place during the 20th century.

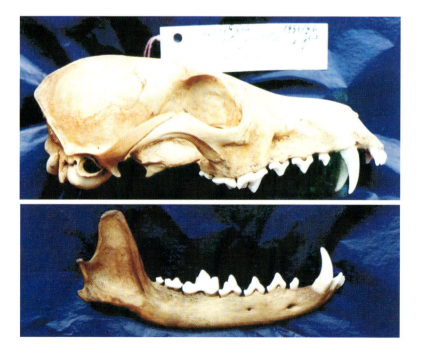

Photo 22.3. Skull of the red fox from a lateral view. Photo by Karol Zub.

Generally, in carnivorous mammals, teeth with the most complicated form and higher adjustment in size and shape are in the central part of the cheek tooth row. This region contains the carnassials and first upper molar. In more specialised, meat-eating carnivores, the properties of teeth in this region are more advanced. However, in the dentition of the red fox, the situation is different. This is because foxes are opportunistic predators. Ecological studies conducted in various countries indicate that during the 20th century, foxes shifted their diets to a more frequent consumption of garbage and carcasses. This trend is reflected in the dental pattern of foxes.

In a population we often observe several variants in shape of the same tooth. These variants are called morphotypes. The carnassials have the most complicated form of a tooth crown, therefore as many as seven kinds of morphotypes were found for this tooth pair. For example, the upper carnassial (i.e. the fourth upper premolar) has four kinds of morphotypes. One of them describes a variation in the crown outline on the buccal side of the tooth (Figure 22.1). The distribution frequencies of morphotypes in a population show definite morphological patterns. However, these patterns can change with time. During the last century, the frequency of the simplest and the most complicated variants of the above morphotype decreased, while the share of the middle variant increased (Figure 22.1). In the red fox

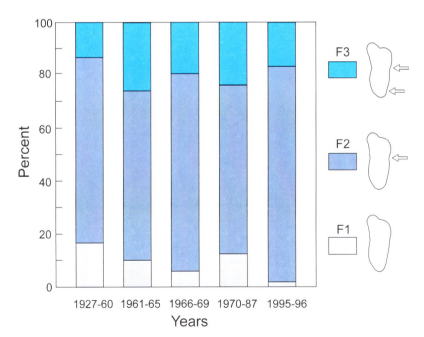

Figure 22.1. Frequency distribution of morphotype F for fourth upper premolar in the red fox during the 20th century.

dentition, the tooth crown in the posterior premolars (i.e. fourth upper premolar, and third and fourth lower premolars) and the third upper incisor become more complex. Other teeth, such as the first molars (centrally situated in the cheek tooth row), the last lower molar, and the first premolars (peripherally situated in the cheek tooth row) did not show any distinct trend in the tooth shape during the same period.

Furthermore, during the 20th century changes in the correlation and variation patterns in the red fox dentition were observed. The correlation coefficient measures the strength of a relationship between certain characteristics, such as tooth size. Higher correlation values indicate a stronger relationship between these characteristics. In the red fox, the correlation relating to sizes of opposing canines and neighbouring first and second upper incisors markedly increased. On the other hand, in the carnassials this correlation of tooth size become less pronounced. The pair of carnassials (fourth upper premolar and first lower molar), the neighbouring fourth lower premolar and first lower molar, the opposite first lower premolar and second upper premolar, and the first and second lower incisors showed a decrease in correlation for tooth size.

These changes suggest that, in the dental system of red foxes, the evolutionary balance has shifted: in the past, foxes' teeth were selected primarily for eating, but now they are being more strongly selected for use in social interactions.

Suggested readings

Hillson S. 1986. Teeth, Cambridge Manuals in Archaeology [2]. Cambridge University Press, Cambridge: I–XIX, 1–376.

Pucek Z. (ed) 1981. Keys to vertebrates of Poland. Mammals. Polish Scientific Publisher, Warszawa: I–VII, 1–367.

Szuma E. 2000. Variation and correlation patterns in the dentition of the red fox from Poland. Annales Zoologici Fennici 37: 113–127.

Szuma E. 2002. Dental polymorphism in a population of the red fox (*Vulpes vulpes*) from Poland. Journal of Zoology, London 256: 243–253.

Szuma E. 2003. Microevolutionary trends in the dentition of the red fox (*Vulpes vulpes*). Journal of Zoological Systematics and Evolutionary Research 41: 47–56.

23

Mammal Research Institute in Białowieża

Krzysztof Niedziałkowski

With 50 years of experience in research on all aspects of mammalian biology and the many projects conducted in Białowieża Primeval Forest, the Mammal Research Institute of the Polish Academy of Sciences is looking forward to new opportunities created by Poland's accession to the European Union. The Institute is open to broad international co-operation and exchange of scientists, it offers professional education for students, and has become involved in regional development, based on science, education, and biodiversity conservation.

The past

The Mammal Research Institute (MRI) was founded in 1952 by Professor August Dehnel as a field station for the Department of Comparative Anatomy of Vertebrates at Marie Curie-Skłodowska University in Lublin. In April 1954, it changed its affiliation to become a branch of the Institute of Zoology of Polish Academy of Sciences. Since 1957, the Mammal Research Institute has been an independent research unit of the Polish Academy of Sciences.

The development of the Institute in the pioneer years was stimulated by the already existing collection of small mammals, originating from the Białowieża National Park. The highlights of MRI's early years were studies on the morphology and histology of shrews which led to the discovery (by A. Dehnel and Z. Pucek) of size and mass recession in shrews during winter, later known as the

Dehnel Effect. Since the 1960's, MRI has been scientifically supervising the reintroduction programme of European bison conducted by the Białowieża National Park. Long-term research on bison addressed the problems of physiology, morphology, disease and ecology of the free-living population in Białowieża Primeval Forest. In the 1960's and 1970's, MRI participated in the International Biological Programme and conducted studies on bioenergetics and ecology of small mammals. The major contributions of the period to the advancement of science were the data on metabolism of various species, energy flow through populations, and standardised techniques of sampling mammalian densities.

The 1980's were marked by the publication of two important books *Keys to Vertebrates of Poland – Mammals* and *Atlas of Polish Mammals*, both co-authored by several MRI staff members. Based on multiple-year censuses over the whole of Poland (carried out during summer expeditions), those two books played an invaluable role in educating a new generation of mammalogists. In 1988, long-term research on the hybridisation of European bison and domestic cattle was completed. Both the basic and applied studies included the effects of cross-breeding the two genera on the reproduction of hybrids, their postnatal development, heredity of parental traits and the perspectives of a wide-scale economical use of hybrids. The results of these experiments were described in the monograph *Hybrids of European bison and domestic cattle* by M. Krasińska. Long-term studies conducted in the pristine forests of Białowieża National Park are another of MRI's specialities. The longest a series with over 40 years of data on small mammal fluctuations in relation to the seed crop of forest trees is the best known example. It has stimulated new research projects as well as re-analyses of existing data on forest rodents in the temperate zones of Europe and North America.

After the political changes in 1989, the staff took advantage of the new system of competitive grants from both national (National Committee of Scientific Research) and international sources (Germany, The Netherlands, Great Britain, U.S.A.). The last decade of the 20th century witnessed a substantial broadening of the research profile of MRI to include genetics, community ecology, and modern conservation biology, as well as a rapid modernisation of the working environment and application of high-tech equipment. Radio-telemetry in field studies of population biology, electrophoresis on cellulose acetate plates in studies of allozyme variation of mammals, infrared video-recording in behavioural studies and advance computer programmes for data analysis and presentation – to mention some examples – made it possible to gain new momentum in research.

In 1998, the *Evolution of Shrews*, edited by J. M. Wójcik and M. Wolsan, with chapters by 22 authors from 11 countries, was published. The book '*provides excellent summaries of recent advances in the biology of shrews and reflects on new directions for future research*', commented the reviewer in Journal of Mammalogy (80, 1999). '*A showcase for shrews*', as praised by Trends in Ecology and Evolution (14, 1999).

With a broad focus on vertebrate predator ecology and other parallel studies (e.g. the long-term monitoring of small mammals and ungulates), the community ecology of 30 species of carnivores and birds of prey was summarised in a book *Predation in vertebrate communities. The Białowieża Primeval Forest as a case study* (B. Jędrzejewska and W. Jędrzejewski, Springer Verlag, Berlin, 1998). The authors analysed and quantified the role of predation in limiting or regulating the prey populations of a wide range of taxa. '*An outstanding piece of work*', complimented a reviewer in Ecology (80, 1999), '*I am aware of no other work of similar scope*'. The book has received Poland's second most prestigious award in science, the Prime Minister's Award for Scientific Achievement (1999).

Since the foundation of MRI in 1952, the scientists working at MRI have published 18 books and 1430 papers, articles, and research reports. The list of international journals in which these papers have been published comprises over 60 titles and includes some of the world's best periodicals in biology, zoology, ecology, and conservation.

Though rather small, growing from 2 scientists in 1954 to 19 in 2003, MRI continues to attract creative and highly motivated young researchers. Since 1952, 35 Polish and 3 foreign students have completed PhD projects at MRI. Habilitation theses (associate professorship dissertations according to the national system of scientific degrees) were received by 10 junior researchers. Currently in April 2004, MRI has 41 permanent staff, including 19 scientists (Photo 23.1). The director's position at MRI has been occupied by Prof. Dr. August Dehnel (1952–1962), Prof. Dr. Zdzisław Pucek (1962–1999), and Dr. habil. Jan M. Wójcik (from 1999). For over 50 years, MRI has hosted and co-operated with many outstanding scientists from Poland and abroad.

Since 1954, the Mammal Research Institute has been editing *Acta Theriologica* (AT), a quarterly international (English language) journal, devoted to all aspects of mammalian biology (Editor-in--Chief: Zdzisław Pucek). AT publishes original research reports, review papers, and book reviews. The subjects covered include: ecology, behaviour, bioenergetics, morphology, reproduction, nutrition, and evolution of mammals. AT has published papers by authors from 59 countries, and is indexed in, among others, Current Contents, Biological Abstracts, Ecological Abstracts, and Referativnyi Zhurnal. The Impact Factor of AT has increased from 0.1 in the late 1980's to 0.945 in 2002.

The mammal collection at MRI includes skulls, skeletons, and (in smaller numbers) skins of mammals, as well as complete specimens of small species stored in formalin or alcohol, gathered during the period 1946–2002. With its total stock reaching 184,500 mammalian specimens, the MRI collection is among the five largest mammal collections in Europe. It is fully available to outside scientists (Polish and foreign researchers) and has been used for comparative research in mammalian morphology, taxonomy, evolution, and more recently, in genetics.

Photo 23.1. The staff of the Mammal Research Institute, Polish Academy of Sciences in Białowieża in 2004. Photo by Karol Zub.

Worth acknowledging also is the expertise and contribution of MRI to the practical aspects of nature conservation at the local, regional and national levels. Our staff contributed expert reports regarding new legislation, co-authored the national strategies for protection of endangered mammal species, supervised the reintroduction of free-living populations of the European bison, and participated in the campaign to enlarge Białowieża National Park.

The present and the future

In 2002, a newly constructed building with excellent facilities was opened (Photo 23.2). In the same year, MRI was awarded the status of the European Union's Centre of Excellence in Biodiversity Conservation and Mammal Research – BIOTER. The BIOTER project (2002–2005) is supported by the European Commission under the Fifth Framework Programme contributing to the implementation of the Key Action "Global Change, Climate and Biodiversity" within the Energy, Environment and Sustainable Development Programme. The Centre of Excellence has several fields of activity: education, research, integration with the European Research Area, development of local awareness by educating in biodiversity issues, co-operation with the local authorities, national parks, and conservation organisations.

In the framework of the BIOTER project, the Mammal Research Institute offers high-level education and training for graduate students from Polish and European universities in Summer Schools in Ecology and Biodiversity and individual, long-term training programmes. Participants have an opportunity to gain hands-on experience in field research methods on mammals and practical aspects of endangered species conservation.

Many of the recently performed and ongoing research projects on mammals are presented in this book. Some of them are long-term projects to be continued in the future. In addition, the MRI staff are currently undertaking new tasks and developing new specialized areas of research. These include the application of geographic information systems, mathematical modelling, and molecular genetics in ecology, conservation biology, and biodiversity studies. The array of species studied and questions asked will broaden, and the geographical coverage of the projects will expand.

In 2003, MRI commenced the European Bison Programme, a new initiative reaching beyond a purely scientific field. Centering on the hallmark animal of North-Eastern Poland, the programme will attempt to combine nature conservation and sustainable development in the region. Various measures will be undertaken to create optimal habitat possibilities for the bison to expand its range towards woodlands surrounding Białowieża Forest. In addition, there are plans to enhance the attractiveness of the region by creating the *European Bison Land*, a coherent touristic product. In the years to come, the European Bison Programme will be carried out jointly by several institutions from the region, including regional authorities.

We hope that in the future, the Mammal Research Institute will continue to benefit from its unique location: in a beautiful, wooden village with friendly people and rich traditions, in the heart of Europe's best preserved lowland forest. On a broader scale, our location at the borderland of Poland and Belarus gives us a great opportunity to bridge the gap between Western and Eastern European scientists.

Photo 23.2. The new laboratory facilities of the Mammal Research Institute. Photo by Karol Zub.

Appendix

English and Latin names of plants, invertebrates, fish, amphibians, reptiles, birds, and mammals mentioned in the book.

Plants

Alder, Black alder	*Alnus glutinosa*
Ash	*Fraxinus excelsior*
Aspen	*Populus tremula*
Beech	*Fagus silvatica*
Birch	*Betula* sp.
Bird cherry	*Prunus padus*
Blueberry	*Vaccinium myrtillus*
Buttercup	*Ranunculus lanuginosus*
Carob fruit	*Ceratonia siliqua*
Citrus	*Citrus* sp.
Elm	*Ulmus scabra*
Fig	*Ficus carica*
Garden thistle	*Cirsium oleraceum*
Goat willow	*Salix caprea*
Goutweed	*Aegopodium podagraria*
Gray willow	*Salix cinerea*
Hairy sedge	*Carex hirta*
Hazel	*Corylus avellana*
Hornbeam	*Carpinus betulus*
Large-leaved lime	*Tilia platyphyllos*
Lime, Small-leaved lime	*Tilia cordata*
Maple, Norway maple	*Acer platanoides*
Meadowsweet	*Filipendula ulmaria*
Oak, Common oak, English oak	*Quercus robur*
Pine, Scots pine	*Pinus silvestris*
Raspberry	*Rubus idaeus*

Reed	*Phragmites australis*
Reed grass	*Calamagrostis arundinacea*
Rose	*Rosa* spp.
Rowan	*Sorbus aucuparia*
Sedge	*Carex* sp.
Sessile oak	*Quercus sessilis*
Spruce, Norway spruce	*Picea abies*
Stinging nettle	*Urtica dioica*
Sycamore	*Acer pseudoplatanus*
Wood anemone	*Anemone nemorosa*
Wood sedge	*Carex sylvatica*

Invertebrates

Amber snail	*Succinea* sp.
Beetles	*Coleoptera*
Bugs	*Hemiptera*
Caterpillars	*Lepidoptera*
Crustaceans	*Crustacea*
Daddy-long-legs	*Opilionida*
Earthworms	*Allobophora* sp., *Dendrobaena* sp., *Lumbricus* sp.
Flies	*Diptera*
Fly larvae	*Calliphora* sp.
Freshwater hog louse	*Asellus* sp.
Freshwater shrimp	*Gammarus* sp.
Mealworm	*Tenebrio molitor*
Mites	*Acarina*
Snails	*Gastropoda*
Spiders	*Aranea*

Fish

Bleak	*Alburnus alburnus*
Gudgeon	*Gobio* sp.
Leucaspius fish	*Leucaspius delineatus*
Roach	*Rutilus rutilus*
Stickleback	*Gasterosteus aculeatus*
Tench	*Tinca tinca*

Amphibians

Common frog	*Rana temporaria*
Common toad	*Bufo bufo*
Frog	*Rana* sp.
Moor frog	*Rana arvalis*
Toad	*Bufo* sp.
Tree frog	*Hyla arborea*

Birds

Blackbird	*Turdus merula*
Black grouse	*Tetrao tetrix*
Blue tit	*Parus caeruleus*
Capercaillie	*Tetrao urogallus*
Chaffinch	*Fringilla coelebs*
Collared flycatcher	*Ficedula albicollis*
Common buzzard	*Buteo buteo*
Crested tit	*Parus cristatus*
Dunnock	*Prunella modularis*
Golden eagle	*Aquila chrysaetos*
Goshawk	*Accipiter gentilis*
Great spotted woodpecker	*Dendrocopos major*
Great tit	*Parus major*
Hawk owl	*Surnia ulula*
Hazel hen	*Bonasa bonasia*
Hobby	*Falco subbuteo*
Crow	*Corvus corone*
Jay	*Garrulus glandarius*
Lesser-spotted eagle	*Aquila pomarina*
Lesser spotted woodpecker	*Dendrocopos minor*
Long-eared owl	*Asio otus*
Magpie	*Pica pica*
Marsh tit	*Parus palustris*
Middle spotted woodpecker	*Dendrocopos medius*
Nuthatch	*Sitta europaea*
Pied flycatcher	*Ficedula hypoleuca*
Pygmy owl	*Glaucidium passerinum*
Raven	*Corvus corax*
Robin	*Erithacus rubecula*
Rough-legged buzzard	*Buteo lagopus*

Snowy owl	*Nyctea scandiaca*
Sparrowhawk	*Accipiter nisus*
Starling	*Sturnus vulgaris*
Tawny owl	*Strix aluco*
Tengmalm's owl	*Aegolius funereus*
Three-toed woodpecker	*Picoides tridactylus*
Thrush	*Turdus* sp.
Tit	*Parus* sp.
White-tailed eagle	*Haliaeetus albicilla*
Willow grouse	*Lagopus lagopus*
Woodcock	*Scolopax rusticola*
Wood warbler	*Phylloscopus sibilatrix*
Wren	*Troglodytes troglodytes*
Yellowhammer	*Emberiza citrinella*

Mammals

American mink	*Mustela vison*
American pygmy shrew	*Sorex hoyi*
Auroch	*Bos primigenius*
Badger	*Meles meles*
Bank vole	*Clethrionomys glareolus*
Barbastelle	*Barbastella barbastellus*
Beaver, Eurasian beaver	*Castor fiber*
Bi-coloured white-toothed shrew	*Crocidura leucodon*
Birch mouse, Northern birch mouse	*Sicista betulina*
Blue whale	*Balaenoptera musculus*
Brandt's bat	*Myotis brandtii*
Brown bear	*Ursus arctos*
Brown hare	*Lepus europaeus*
Brown long-eared bat	*Plecotus auritus*
Brown rat	*Rattus norvegicus*
Camel	*Camelus* sp.
Cattle	*Bos taurus*
Cave lion	*Panthera spelaea*
Chamois	*Rupicapra rupicapra*
Common dormouse	*Muscardinus avellanarius*
Common mole	*Talpa europea*
Common pipistrelle	*Pipistrellus pipistrellus*
Common shrew	*Sorex araneus*
Common vole	*Microtus arvalis*

Daubenton's bat	*Myotis daubentonii*
Dog	*Canis familiaris*
Eastern hedgehog	*Erinaceus concolor*
Eurasian water shrew	*Neomys fodiens*
European bison	*Bison bonasus*
European mink	*Mustela lutreola*
Fat dormouse	*Glis glis*
Field vole	*Microtus agrestis*
Forest dormouse	*Dryomys nitedula*
Giant deer	*Megaceros giganteus*
Ground sloth	*Eremotherium laurillardi*
Hare	*Lepus* sp.
Harvest mouse	*Micromys minutus*
Horse	*Equus caballus*
House mouse	*Mus musculus*
Indian elephant	*Elephas maximus*
Leisler's bat	*Nyctalus leisleri*
Lynx	*Lynx lynx*
Mammoth	*Mammuthus primigenius*
Masked shrew	*Sorex caecutiens*
Mediterranean water shrew	*Neomys anomalus*
Moose	*Alces alces*
Mountain hare	*Lepus timidus*
Musk deer	*Moschus moschiferus*
Nathusius' pipistrelle	*Pipistrellus nathusii*
Natterer's bat	*Myotis nattereri*
Noctule	*Nyctalus noctula*
Northern bat	*Eptesicus nilssonii*
Otter	*Lutra lutra*
Parti-coloured bat	*Vespertilio murinus*
Pine marten	*Martes martes*
Pine vole	*Microtus subterraneus*
Polar bear	*Ursus maritimus*
Polecat	*Mustela putorius*
Pygmy shrew	*Sorex minutus*
Pygmy white-toothed shrew	*Suncus etruscus*
Raccoon dog	*Nyctereutes procyonides*
Red deer	*Cervus elaphus*
Red fox	*Vulpes vulpes*
Red squirrel, Squirrel	*Sciurus vulgaris*
Roe deer	*Capreolus capreolus*
Root vole	*Microtus oeconomus*

Serotine	*Eptesicus serotinus*
Sika deer	*Cervus nippon*
Steppe bison	*Bison priscus*
Stoat	*Mustela erminea*
Stone marten	*Martes foina*
Striped field mouse	*Apodemus agrarius*
Valais shrew	*Sorex antinorii*
Water vole	*Arvicola terrestris*
Weasel	*Mustela nivalis*
White-backed woodpacker	*Dendrocopos leucotos*
Wild boar	*Sus scrofa*
Wolf	*Canis lupus*
Woolly rhinoceros	*Coelodonta antiquitatis*
Wolverine	*Gulo gulo*
Woodchuck	*Marmota monax*
Wood mouse	*Apodemus sylvaticus*
Yellow-necked mouse	*Apodemus flavicollis*

Authors' profiles and addresses

Kamil Bartoń graduated from the Jagiellonian University in Kraków. Since 2003, as a junior researcher at the Mammal Research Institute Polish Academy of Sciences (MRI PAS), he has begun his PhD project on the impact of food and predation on the microtine rodents of open habitats, in a gradient of ecosystem productivity. He is also interested in ecological mathematical modelling.
(Mammal Research Institute, PAS, 17-230 Białowieża, Poland;
 kbarton@bison.zbs.bialowieza.pl)

Dr Katarzyna Daleszczyk, a junior scientist at MRI, has participated in research on the relationships between ecology and morphology for several bat species. In 2003, she completed her PhD on the breeding behaviour of European bison in Białowieża Primeval Forest. Her main interests are the behaviour, ecology, and conservation of European bison. Currently, she participates in projects on habitat utilisation and reproductive strategies of bison.
(Mammal Research Institute PAS, 17-230 Białowieża, Poland;
 kdalesz@bison.zbs.bialowieza.pl)

Prof. dr habil. Joanna Gliwicz is a specialist in animal ecology and conservation biology. She has published over 120 scientific papers, book chapters and articles. For many years she has been a lecturer in ecology, vertebrate zoology, and animal behavior at Warsaw Agricultural University and the College of Ecology and Management in Warsaw. Currently, she is affiliated with the Museum and Institute of Zoology of the Polish Academy of Sciences. Her recent interests and studies concern landscape ecology, population ecology and behaviour of small mammals, as well as factors shaping local and global biodiversity.
(Museum and Institute of Zoology, PAS, Wilcza 64, 00-679 Warsaw, Poland;
 gliwicz@miiz.waw.pl)

Dr Elżbieta Jancewicz is the assistant professor of the Forestry Faculty at the Warsaw Agricultural University. Her research interests cover small mammal ecology and the feeding and spatial behavior of shrews and

rodents. In 2002, she completed her PhD thesis on the spatial behaviour of the root vole in river valleys of Białowieża Forest.
(Department of Forest Protection and Ecology, Warsaw Agricultural University, Nowoursynowska 159, 02-776 Warsaw, Poland; Elzbieta.Jancewicz@wl.sggw.waw.pl)

Dr Bogdan Jaroszewicz, Deputy Director of the Białowieża National Park, is responsible for science and education, and conducted his PhD research on the taxonomic status of a rare butterfly *Carterocephalus palaemon tolli* inhabiting Białowieża Primeval Forest. He is interested in taxonomy, ecology and conservation of butterflies. He co-authored and edited the book *Catalogue of the fauna of Białowieża Primeval Forest* (Warsaw 2001).
(Białowieża National Park, 17-230 Białowieża, Poland; jarosz@bpn.com.pl)

Prof. dr habil. Bogumiła Jędrzejewska, a senior scientist at MRI, conducts studies in animal ecology, forest ecology, and conservation biology, in particular on the roles of climate, food, and predation in shaping population dynamics of mammals in Białowieża Forest. She is the author and editor of 2 scientific books and 80 papers and articles. At the MRI, she is a leader of the Research Group *Ecology of Natural Ecosystems*. Her recent interests include cascading effects in food chains, and biogeographic variation in the life habits of European mammals and birds.
(Mammal Research Institute PAS, 17-230 Białowieża, Poland; bjedrzej@bison.zbs.bialowieza.pl)

Prof. dr habil. Włodzimierz Jędrzejewski, Deputy Director for Science at MRI, has been conducting studies on animal ecology (predator-prey relationships, population regulation), forest ecology, and conservation biology. He is a leading specialist in predation ecology and forest-ungulate-predator interactions, having conducted research on ecology of wolves, lynxes, weasels, and red deer in Białowieża Primeval Forest. W. Jędrzejewski is the author of one scientific book and 80 papers and articles. His current projects focus on the role of large predators in limiting ungulate numbers, factors shaping the fluctuations of small rodents in the European temperate zone, population genetics and migration corridors of wolves and other large mammals in Poland and Europe.
(Mammal Research Institute PAS, 17-230 Białowieża, Poland; wjedrzej@bison.zbs.bialowieza.pl)

Dr Jan F. Kamler has studied the ecology and relationships of swift foxes, coyotes, bobcats, raccoons, and opossums in Kansas and Texas, USA. In 2002, he received his PhD degree from the Texas Tech University in Lubbock, USA. In 2002–2004, as a recipient of the Fulbright Student Scholarship and a postdoctoral researcher at the MRI, he conducted a study on the ecology of red deer in Białowieża Primeval Forest.
(Mammal Research Institute PAS, 17-230 Białowieża, Poland; jkamler@bison.zbs.bialowieza.pl and jankamler@hotmail.com)

Dr habil. Marek Konarzewski is a senior researcher at the MRI and associate professor at the University of Białystok. In 1991-1993, he was a postdoctoral fellow at the University of California in Los Angeles, USA. He has published over 40 scientific papers and articles. Research interests of M. Konarzewski cover ecological and evolutionary studies of birds and mammals, especially in the field of physiological ecology and evolutionary physiology. His research projects carried out at MRI are aimed to unravel physiological mechanisms of the evolution of life history traits.
(Institute of Biology, University of Białystok, Świerkowa 20 B, 15-950 Białystok, and Mammal Research Institute PAN, 17-230 Białowieża, Poland; marekk@uwb.edu.pl)

Dr Rafał Kowalczyk, junior scientist at MRI, completed a PhD on the ecology of European badgers in Białowieża Primeval Forest in 2001. His research interests encompass also carnivore (lynx, wolf) ecology and the influences of introduced predators (raccoon dog, American mink) on native fauna. Currently, he is involved in studies on the reproductive strategy of European bison and population genetics of the lynx.
(Mammal Research Institute PAS, 17-230 Białowieża, Poland; rkowal@bison.zbs.bialowieza.pl)

Dr habil. Małgorzata Krasińska, a senior scientist at MRI and a leader of the Research Group *Ecology of European Bison*, is a specialist in the biology and management of European bison. She has conducted several projects on various aspects of morphology, conservation biology, life habitats and space use of the free-living bison populations in Poland and the Belarus Republic. In 1961-1976, she conducted a hybridisation experiment with domestic cattle and European bison. She is the author of over 90 scientific papers and articles.
(Mammal Research Institute PAS, 17-230 Białowieża, Poland; mkrasin@bison.zbs.bialowieza.pl)

Dr Zbigniew A. Krasiński, doctor of veterinary sciences, is a specialist in disease of wild animals. A scientist affiliated with the Białowieża National Park, he has been monitoring the numbers of free-living populations of European bison, and conducting studies on their breeding biology, recovery, and conservation. Besides numerous scientific papers, he has been a productive writer of popular articles and books about the bison, and a keen photographer of bison in the wild.
(Białowieża National Park, 17-230 Białowieża, Poland; bpn@bpn.com.pl)

Prof. dr habil. Stanisław Miścicki is a lecturer in the Forestry Faculty at the Warsaw Agricultural University. His main research interest lies in the area of forest management, interpretation of aerial photographs, forest inventory, management planning, development of natural forests, and ungulate impacts on forest regeneration. In his Habilitation thesis (1996), S. Miścicki elaborated a method of control and assessment of ungulate damage

to young stands and forest regeneration. His current research is focused on developments in forest regeneration – especially in national parks, including the Białowieża National Park.
(Department of Forest Management, Geomatics and Forest Economics, Warsaw Agricultural University, Nowoursynowska 159, 02-776 Warsaw, Poland; miscicki@delta.sggw.waw.pl)

Magdalena Niedziałkowska graduated from the University of Warsaw in 2002. Since 2003, as a junior researcher at MRI, she has begun her PhD study on the influence of habitat isolation and productivity on species and genetic diversity of mammals in woodlands of north-eastern Poland.
(Mammal Research Institute PAS, 17-230 Białowieża, Poland; mrogala@bison.zbs.bialowieza.pl)

Krzysztof Niedziałkowski graduated from the Warsaw School of Economics in 2002. Since 2003, he has been affiliated with MRI as an administrative coordinator of the European Bison Programme. His research interests focus on the economic aspects of nature conservation.
(Mammal Research Institute PAS, 17-230 Białowieża, Poland; kniedz@bison.zbs.bialowieza.pl)

Prof. dr habil. Zdzisław Pucek, a former Director of MRI (in 1963-1999), has been a senior scientist at MRI and the Editor-in-Chief of *Acta Theriologica*. His main fields of research are biomorphology of mammals (in particular, the seasonal and age-related changes in shrews and the postnatal development of rodents), ecology (population dynamics of mammals and methods of estimating population density), faunistic research and protection of mammals, and conservation strategies for the European bison. Z. Pucek is a full member of the Polish Academy of Sciences. He is the author and editor of 6 scientific books, 20 book chapters, and nearly 200 papers and articles.
(Mammal Research Institute PAS, 17-230 Białowieża, Poland; zpucek@bison.zbs.bialowieza.pl)

Dr Ireneusz Ruczyński is a junior scientist at MRI. His research interests cover ecology, biodiversity, behaviour and conservation of bats. In 2003, he completed a PhD study on the roosting ecology and behavior of forest-dwelling bats in Białowieża Forest. Currently, he is participating in a project on interspecific competition and niche separation in soricine shrews.
(Mammal Research Institute PAS, 17-230 Białowieża, Poland; iruczyns@bison.zbs.bialowieza.pl)

Dr Leszek Rychlik, a junior scientist at MRI, is interested in behavioural ecology and evolution of small mammals, mainly shrews. His PhD study, completed in 1995, concerned the foraging behaviour of water shrews. The ongoing studies of L. Rychlik address the questions of intra- and interspecific competition and niche separation in shrews, morphological

and behavioural shifts under competitive release, and phylogeography of water shrews in Europe.
(Mammal Research Institute PAS, 17-230 Białowieża, Poland; lrychlik@bison.zbs.bialowieza.pl)

Tomasz Samojlik graduated from the Marie Curie-Skłodowska University in Lublin. Since 2002, he has been an administrative coordinator of the European Union's Centre of Excellence BIOTER at MRI. He has begun his PhD, studying the environmental history of Białowieża Primeval Forest.
(Mammal Research Institute PAS, 17-230 Białowieża, Poland; samojlik@bison.zbs.bialowieza.pl)

Dr Krzysztof Schmidt, a junior scientist at MRI, conducted his PhD study, completed in 1999, on the population ecology and behaviour of the Eurasian lynx and its impact on roe deer and red deer in Białowieża Primeval Forest. He was also involved in research on wolf ecology, and conducted a joint project with Japanese researchers on the movements and activity of the Iriomote cat (on Iriomote Island, Japan). Currently, he is investigating population genetics of the lynx.
(Mammal Research Institute PAS, 17-230 Białowieża, Poland; kschmidt@bison.zbs.bialowieza.pl)

Nuria Selva has been conducting her PhD study on the role of scavenging in the predator community of Białowieża Primeval Forest (MRI, Poland and University of Sevilla, Spain). Her main research interests include predator ecology, conservation, and ecological modelling.
(Mammal Research Institute PAS, 17-230 Białowieża, Poland; nuria@bison.zbs.bialowieza.pl)

Krystyna Stachura graduated from the Marie Curie-Skłodowska University in Lublin. Since 2003, as a junior researcher at MRI, she has begun her PhD study on roe deer population ecology in relation to habitat productivity. She is interested in the application of geographic information systems in ecology and conservation biology.
(Mammal Research Institute PAS, 17-230 Białowieża, Poland; kstach@bison.zbs.bialowieza.pl)

Dr Elwira Szuma is a junior scientist at MRI, with her main research interests in the morphology and evolution of carnivores. Her PhD study, completed in 1999, concerned ontogenetic and evolutionary implications of metric and non-metric tooth variation in the Polish population of the red fox. Current research of E. Szuma is focused on geographic variation in the dental system of the red fox.
(Mammal Research Institute PAS, 17-230 Białowieża, Poland; eszuma@bison.zbs.bialowieza.pl)

Dr Małgorzata Tokarska received her PhD degree from the Agricultural University in Wrocław in 1999. Her doctoral study concerned polymorphism of the alpha S1 casein gene in goats. Since 2003, she has been affiliated with MRI as a junior scientist. Her current scientific activities are focused on non-tissue specific patterns of gene expression, and population and ecological genetics in mammals, including the European bison.
(Mammal Research Institute PAS, 17-230 Białowieża, Poland; tokarska@bison.zbs.bialowieza.pl)

Dr habil. Jan Marek Wójcik is the Director of the Mammal Research Institute and a leader of the Research Group *Genetics and Behavioural Ecology of Mammals*. His main research interests are in the fields of population genetics and evolution of mammals. He has conducted research on chromosome and protein variations and karyotype evolution in common shrews. In 1990–1991, he was a postdoctoral fellow of the British Council at Oxford University, Great Britain. He is the author and editor of 2 books and 58 scientific papers and articles.
(Mammal Research Institute PAS, 17-230 Białowieża, Poland; jwojcik@bison.zbs.bialowieza.pl)

Dr Anna Maria Wójcik, a junior scientist at MRI, is interested in population genetics and morphometric and non-metric variations of mammals. Her PhD study, completed in 1990, analysed factors responsible for the maintenance of protein polymorphism in a population of the yellow-necked mouse. Her ongoing studies are focused on DNA variation in the European bison and other mammals.
(Mammal Research Institute PAS, 17-230 Białowieża, Poland; awojcik@bison.zbs.bialowieza.pl)

Dr Andrzej Zalewski, a junior scientist at MRI, has been conducting studies on ecology (social systems, feeding habits, competition, and population regulation) and conservation of carnivores, especially mustelids. In 1998, he completed his PhD project on the ecology of pine martens in Białowieża National Park. His current research is focused on space use and reproduction strategies in solitary carnivores, and the influence of introduced American mink on native fauna.
(Mammal Research Institute PAS, 17-230 Białowieża, Poland; zalewski@bison.zbs.bialowieza.pl)

Karol Zub graduated from the University of Białystok in 2002. As a junior researcher at MRI, he is interested in the ecology and conservation biology of raptors and small carnivores. He has begun his PhD study on the population dynamics, genetic variability, and physiology of weasels in relation to their body size variation.
(Mammal Research Institute PAS, 17-230 Białowieża, Poland; karolzub@bison.zbs.bialowieza.pl)